English Grammar for Students of Spanish

The Study Guide
for Those Learning Spanish

Seventh edition

Emily Spinelli
University of Michigan-Dearborn
Executive Director, American Association of Teachers
of Spanish and Portuguese

The Olivia and Hill Press®

THE O&H STUDY GUIDES
Jacqueline Morton, editor

English Grammar for Students of Spanish
English Grammar for Students of French
English Grammar for Students of German
English Grammar for Students of Italian
English Grammar for Students of Latin
English Grammar for Students of Russian
English Grammar for Students of Japanese
English Grammar for Students of Arabic
English Grammar for Students of Chinese
Gramática española para estudiantes de inglés

Printed in the U.S.A.

ISBN: 978-0-934034-41-8

Library of Congress Control Number: 2011945967

CONTENTS

CONTENTS

CONTENTS

STUDY TIPS

English Grammar for Students of Spanish explains the grammatical terms that are in your Spanish textbook and shows you how they relate to English grammar. Once you understand the terms and concepts in your own language, it will be easier for you to understand what is being introduced in your textbook and by your teacher. To help you become a more efficient language learner, we offer specific *Study Tips* for learning different types of words.

TIPS FOR LEARNING GRAMMAR

Grammar is one of the tools you need to communicate orally and in writing. Linking a grammar point with its purpose will make grammar more meaningful for you and will help you recall what you have learned.

To learn grammar points — Most textbooks indicate the purpose of the grammar point being introduced either in the title or subtitle of the grammar section, or within the first paragraph.

For example:

> Title — Descriptive adjectives
> Purpose — Describing family and friends

In other words, you will need to learn how to form and use descriptive adjectives so that you can describe family and friends. Although only the description of people is mentioned in the purpose above, examples in the chapter will extend the use of descriptive adjectives to other situations, such as describing animals and things. You should make note of these additional uses.

The following is a list of some important grammar points and their purpose.

Nouns and definite articles
Talking about specific people and things

Present tense
Talking about everyday activities; discussing what we do

Past tense
Talking about past activities; narrating in the past

Future tense
Talking about what we will do; narrating in the future

Conditional
Explaining what we would do under certain conditions

Formal and familiar commands
Giving instructions and orders

Reflexive verbs
Discussing daily routine

Demonstrative adjectives
Pointing out people and things

Interrogative adjectives
Asking questions

Possessive adjectives
Indicating ownership

Comparison of adjectives
Comparing people and comparing things

Subject pronouns
Addressing and referring to people

Here are some suggestions to help you make the connection between the grammar point and its purpose.

1. As you read the grammar explanations in your textbook, look for the purpose of each grammar point and highlight it.
2. Create a flashcard for each grammar point and indicate its purpose.
3. As you do the grammar exercises and activities, take the time to see how they relate to the purpose of the grammar point being introduced.

Your textbook will provide exercises and activities that allow you to practice the grammar point for various purposes.

Tips for Learning Vocabulary

One aspect of language learning is remembering a number of foreign words.

To learn vocabulary — Flashcards are a good, handy tool for learning new words and their meaning. You can carry flashcards with you, group them as you wish, and add information as you advance. Creating your own flashcards is an important first step in learning vocabulary.

1. Write the Spanish word or expression on one side of an index card and its English equivalent on the other side.

2. On the Spanish side of the card add a short sentence using the word or expression. It will be easier for you to recall a word in context. To make sure that your sentence is grammatically accurate, copy an example from your textbook. For review purposes, write down the chapter and page number of your textbook where the word is introduced.

3. On the Spanish side, include any irregularities and whatever information is relevant to the word in question. You will find specific suggestions under the *Study Tips* sections of this handbook.

4. Many textbooks have an online flashcard feature that is available on the textbook website. The vocabulary lists found within a chapter are set up on digitized flashcards with the English word on one side of the card and the Spanish equivalent on the other. These digitized flashcards can be used on your computer, tablet, or other device. These digital programs usually offer the ability to create new flashcards as the need arises.

5. There are also computer programs that allow you to create flashcards for learning vocabulary.

How to use the cards — Regardless of the side of the card you're working on, always say the Spanish word out loud.

1. Look at the Spanish side first. Going from Spanish to English is easier than going from English to Spanish because it only requires your recognizing the Spanish word. Read the Spanish word(s) out loud, giving the English equivalent; then, check your answer on the English side.

2. When you go easily from Spanish to English, turn the cards to the English side. Going from English to Spanish is harder than going from Spanish to English because you have to pull the word and its spelling out of your memory. Say the Spanish equivalent out loud as you write it down on a separate sheet of paper; then check the spelling with the card. Some students prefer closing their eyes and visualizing the Spanish word and its spelling.

3. As you progress, put aside the cards you know and concentrate on the ones you still do not know.

How to remember words — Below are suggestions to help you associate a Spanish word with an English word with a similar meaning. This is the first step and it will put the Spanish word in your short-term memory. Use and practice, the next step, will put the words in your long-term memory.

1. There are many words, called **COGNATES**, that have the same meaning and approximately the same spelling in English as in Spanish. These words are easy to recognize in Spanish, but you will have to concentrate on the differences in spelling and pronunciation.

English	Spanish
important	importante
problem	problema
visit	visitar

2. Try to associate the Spanish word with an English word that has a related meaning.

Spanish	English	Related English word
el avión	the airplane	aviation
preocupado	worried	preoccupation
el ascensor	the elevator	ascend

3. If the Spanish word has no similarities to English, rely on any association that is meaningful to you. The more associations you have for a word, i.e., the more "hooks," the easier it will be for you to remember it. Different types of associations work for different people. Find the one that works best for you. Here are some suggestions:

- Group words by topic or personal associations – It is easier to learn new words if you group them. You can group them according to topics such as food, clothing, activities you do for fun, sports, school, home, or according to personal associations such as things you carry in your backpack, things you'd take on a desert island, gifts you'd like to receive, etc.

- Associate the word with an image – If you have trouble remembering a particular word, you might want to create a "bizarre image" in your mind using English words with similar sounds with which to associate it. This method is very subjective and only works for some people.

caro = *expensive*
You're giving me an *expensive* **car** 'Oh, boy!'

con = *with*
"He is a **con** man *with* charm."

4. To reinforce the Spanish word and its spelling, use it in a short sentence.

TIPS FOR LEARNING WORD FORMS

170

Another aspect of language learning is remembering the various forms a word can take; for example, another form of *book* is *books* and *do* can take the form of *does* and *did*. As a general rule, the first part of the word indicates its meaning and the second part indicates its form.

To learn forms — The best way to learn new forms is to practice writing them on paper or using a computer or other electronic device. You should write the forms until you get them correct. The following steps will make learning forms easier.

1. Look for a pattern in the different forms of a word.   180
   - Which letters, if any, remain constant?
   - Which letters change?
   - Is there a pattern to the changes?
   - Is this pattern the same as one you already know?
   - If this pattern is similar to one you already know, what are the similarities and differences with the previous pattern?

   We will help you establish patterns in the *Study Tips* at the end of selected chapters.

2. Once you have established the pattern, it will be easy to memorize the forms.   190
   - Write down the forms while saying them out loud.
   - Continue until you are able to write all the forms correctly without referring to your textbook.

3. Write short sentences using the various forms.

To review forms — You can use flashcards to review forms, not to learn them. You will find suggestions on what to write on the cards under the *Study Tips* at the end of selected chapters.

TIPS FOR EFFECTIVE STUDY

200

Before class — Read the sections in *English Grammar for Students of Spanish* and in your textbook that cover the topics you are going to study in class.

In class — Focus on developing your communicative skills by practicing the language with your classmates. Come to class well prepared so you can take full advantage of this classroom practice.

Take notes. This way you will know what the teacher considers important and it will reinforce what you are studying.

Homework — Take notes as you study your textbook. Highlighting is not sufficient. The more often you write down and use vocabulary and rules, the easier it will be for you to remember them. Complete exercises and activities over several short periods of time rather than in one long session.

Written exercises — As you write Spanish words or sentences, say them out loud. Each time you write, read, say, or listen to a word, it reinforces it in your memory.

Objective — You have learned something successfully when you are able to write a short sentence in Spanish using the correct form of the Spanish words without reference to a textbook or a dictionary. The *Study Tips* throughout this handbook will help you with this learning process.

CHAPTER

1

WHAT'S IN A WORD?

When you learn a foreign language, in this case Spanish, you   1
must look at each word in four ways: MEANING, PART OF SPEECH,
FUNCTION, and FORM.

MEANING

An English word may be connected to a Spanish word that
has a similar meaning.

> *House*, a building in which people live, has the same
> meaning as the Spanish word **casa**.

Words with equivalent meanings are learned by memo-   10
rizing VOCABULARY (see pp. 2-5).

Occasionally knowing one Spanish word will help you
learn another.

> Knowing that **niño** means *boy* should help you learn that
> **niña** is *girl*; or knowing that **hermano** is *brother* should
> help you remember that **hermana** is *sister*.

Usually, however, there is little similarity between words
and knowing one Spanish word will not help you learn
another. As a general rule, you must memorize each   20
vocabulary item separately.

> Knowing that **hombre** is *man* will not help you learn that
> **mujer** is *woman*.

In addition, every language has expressions in which the
meaning of a group of words is different from the
meaning of the words taken individually. These are called
IDIOMATIC EXPRESSIONS, or IDIOMS. For instance, *"to fall*
asleep*"* and *"to take* a walk*"* are English expressions where
"to fall" and *"to take"* do not have their usual meaning as
in *"to fall* down the stairs,*"* or *"to take* a book to school.*"*   30
You will have to be on the alert for these idioms because
they cannot be translated word-for-word in Spanish.

> *to fall asleep*   dormirse
> [word-for-word *"to put oneself to sleep"*]
>
> *to take a walk*   dar un paseo
> [word-for-word *"to give a walk"*]

PART OF SPEECH

In English and Spanish words are grouped according to how they are used in a sentence. There are eight groups corresponding to eight PARTS OF SPEECH:

adjectives	nouns
adverbs	pronouns
articles	prepositions
conjunctions	verbs

Some parts of speech are further broken down according to type. Adjectives, for instance, can be descriptive, interrogative, demonstrative, or possessive. Each part of speech has its own rules for spelling, pronunciation, and use.

In order to choose the correct Spanish equivalent of an English word, you will have to identify its part of speech. As an example, look at the word *leaves* in the following two sentences. In each sentence *leaves* belongs to a different part of speech, each one corresponding to a different Spanish word.

John *leaves* the room.

verb → **sale**

John swept the *leaves* off the deck.

noun → **hojas**

The various sections of this handbook show you how to identify parts of speech so that you are able to choose the proper Spanish words and the rules that apply to them.

FUNCTION

In English and Spanish the role a word plays in a sentence is called its FUNCTION. For example, words that are nouns can have the following functions:

subject
direct object
indirect object
object of a preposition

In order to choose the correct Spanish equivalent of an English word, you will have to identify its function. As an example, look at the word *him* in the following two sentences. In each sentence *him* has a different function, each one corresponding to a different Spanish word.

They don't see *him*.

direct object → **lo**

I wrote *him* a letter.

    indirect object → **le**
80

The various sections of this handbook show you how to identify the function of words so that you are able to choose the proper Spanish words and the rules that apply to them.

FORM

In English and in Spanish, a word can influence the form of another word, that is, its spelling and pronunciation. This "matching" is called **AGREEMENT** and it is said that one word "agrees" with another.
90

| I am | *am* agrees with *I* |
| she is | *is* agrees with *she* |

Agreement does not play a big role in English, but it is an important part of the Spanish language. As an example, look at the sentences below where the lines indicate which words must agree with one another.

    *My older **brother** works in that large modern **office**.*

    Mi **hermano** mayor trabaja en esa **oficina** grande y moderna.

In English, the only word that affects another word in the sentence is *brother*, which forces us to say *works*. If we changed *brother* to *brothers*, we would have to say *work* to make it agree with *brothers*.
100

In Spanish, the word for *brother* (**hermano**) not only affects the spelling and pronunciation of *works* (**trabaja**), but also the spelling and pronunciation of the Spanish words for *my* (**mi**) and *older* (**mayor**). The word for *office* (**oficina**) affects the spelling and pronunciation of the Spanish words for *that* (**esa**), *large* (**grande**), and *modern* (**moderna**). If we changed *brother* to *sister* and *office* to *offices* all the affected words would also have to change.
110

As the various parts of speech are introduced in this handbook, we will go over "agreement" so that you learn which words agree with others and how the agreement is shown.

WHAT IS A NOUN?

1   A **NOUN** is a word that can be the name of a person, animal, place, thing, event or idea.

- a person   professor, clown, student, girl, baby
  Professor Smith, Bozo, Bill, Mary
- an animal   elephant, horse, snake, eagle
  Kermit, Bambi, Garfield, Teddy
- a place   theater, restaurant, city, state, country
  Yankee Stadium, Ohio, Mexico City, Peru
- a thing   apple, lamp, dress, airplane, company
  Coca-Cola, iPad, General Motors
- an event   graduation, marriage, birth, Thanksgiving
  or activity   the Olympics, shopping, resting
- an idea   democracy, humor, hatred, honor
  or concept   time, love, justice, jealousy, poverty

As you can see, a noun is not only a word that names something that is tangible (i.e., something you can touch), such as a *lamp, horse* or *iPhone*, it can also be the name of things that are abstract (i.e., that you cannot touch), such as *justice, jealousy*, and *honor.*

A noun that does not state the name of a specific person, place, thing, etc. is called a **COMMON NOUN.** A common noun does not begin with a capital letter, unless it is the first word of a sentence. All the nouns above that are not capitalized are common nouns.

A noun that is the name of a specific person, place, thing, etc. is called a **PROPER NOUN.** A proper noun always begins with a capital letter. All the nouns above that are capitalized are proper nouns.

            Bill is my friend.
            proper common
            noun   noun

A noun that is made up of two words is called a **COMPOUND NOUN.** A compound noun can be composed of two common nouns, such as *comic strip* and *ice cream,* or two proper nouns, such as *South America* or *Mexico City.*

IN ENGLISH

To help you learn to recognize nouns, look at the paragraph below where the nouns are in *italics*.

> The *countries* that make up the Spanish-speaking *world*   40
> export *products* that we use every *day*. *Spain* produces
> many of the *shoes, purses,* and *gloves* that are sold in
> *stores* throughout the *United States*. *Spain* also sells us
> much *wine, sherry,* and *brandy*. The *islands* of the
> *Caribbean* and the *nations* of *Central America* supply us
> with tropical *fruits* such as *bananas* and *melons*; *sugar* is
> another important *export* of these *regions*. While *oil* is a
> major *source* of *income* for *Mexico* and *Venezuela*, the
> *economies* of several other *countries* of *Latin America*
> depend upon the *production* and *exportation* of *coffee*.

50

IN SPANISH

Nouns are identified in the same way as they are in English.

TERMS USED TO TALK ABOUT NOUNS

- GENDER — A noun has a gender; that is, it can be classified according to whether it is masculine, feminine, or neuter (see *What is Meant by Gender?*, p. 12).
- NUMBER — A noun has a number; that is, it can be identified according to whether it is singular or plural (see *What is Meant by Number?*, p. 15).   60
- FUNCTION — A noun can have a variety of functions in a sentence; that is, it can be the subject of the sentence (see *What is a Subject?*, p. 28) or an object (see *What are Objects?*, p. 138.

STUDY TIPS — NOUNS AND THEIR GENDER (SEE P. 20)

CHAPTER

WHAT IS MEANT BY GENDER?

GENDER in the grammatical sense means that a word can be classified as masculine, feminine, or neuter.

> Did Paul give Mary the book?
> Yes, *he* gave *it* to *her*.
> | | |
>   masc. neuter fem.

Grammatical gender is not very important in English; however, it is at the very heart of the Spanish language where the gender of a word is often reflected not only in the way the word itself is spelled and pronounced, but also in the way all the words connected to it are spelled and pronounced.

More parts of speech have a gender in Spanish than in English.

ENGLISH	SPANISH
pronouns	pronouns
possessive adjectives	adjectives
	articles
	nouns

Since each part of speech follows its own rules to indicate gender, you will find gender discussed in the chapters dealing with articles and the various types of pronouns and adjectives. In this section we shall only look at the gender of nouns.

IN ENGLISH

Nouns themselves do not have a gender, but sometimes their meaning will indicate a gender based on the biological sex of the person or animal the noun stands for. For example, when we replace a proper or common noun which refers to a man or a woman, we use *he* for males and *she* for females.

- nouns referring to males indicate the **MASCULINE** gender

> Paul came home; *he* was tired, and I was glad to see *him*.
> | | |
> noun (male)   masculine   masculine

- nouns referring to females indicate the **FEMININE** gender

> Mary came home; *she* was tired, and I was glad to see *her*.
> | | |
> noun (female)   feminine   feminine

All the proper or common nouns that do not have a biological gender are considered **NEUTER** and are replaced by *it*.

The city of Buenos Aires is lovely. I enjoyed visiting *it*.
      noun   neuter

40

IN SPANISH

All nouns — common nouns and proper nouns — have a gender; they are either masculine or feminine. Do not confuse the grammatical terms "masculine" and "feminine" with the terms "male" and "female." Only a few Spanish nouns have a grammatical gender tied to whether they refer to someone of the male or female sex. Most nouns have a gender which must be memorized.

50

The gender of common and proper nouns based on **BIOLOGICAL GENDER** is easy to determine. These are nouns whose meaning can only refer to one or the other of the biological sexes, male or female.

MALES → MASCULINE	FEMALES → FEMININE
Paul	Mary
boy	girl
brother	sister
stepfather	niece

60

The gender of all other nouns, common and proper, cannot be explained or figured out. These nouns have a **GRAMMATICAL GENDER** that is unrelated to biological gender and which must be memorized. Here are some examples of English nouns classified under the gender of their Spanish equivalent.

MASCULINE	FEMININE
money	coin
dress	shirt
country	nation
Peru	Argentina
Wednesday	peace

70

As you learn a new noun, you should always learn its gender because it will affect the spelling and pronunciation of the words related to it. Textbooks and dictionaries usually indicate the gender of a noun with an *m.* for masculine or an *f.* for feminine. Sometimes the definite articles are used: **el** for masculine or **la** for feminine (see *What are Articles?*, p. 17).

ENDINGS INDICATING GENDER

Gender can sometimes be determined by looking at the end of the Spanish noun. In the lists that follow there are endings that often indicate feminine nouns and others that indicate masculine nouns. Since you will encounter many nouns with these endings in basic Spanish, it is certainly worthwhile to familiarize yourself with them.

FEMININE ENDINGS

-a	la casa, la biblioteca	*house, library*
-dad, -tad	la ciudad, la libertad	*city, liberty*
-z	la nariz	*nose*
-ión, -ción	la reunión, la nación	*meeting, nation*
-umbre	la costumbre	*custom*
-ie	la especie	*species*

MASCULINE ENDINGS

Any ending except those provided in the "Feminine endings" list above. In particular:

-l	el papel	*paper*
-o	el libro	*book*
-n	el jardín	*garden*
-e	el parque	*park*
-r	el dolor	*pain*
-s	el interés	*interest*

To help you remember these endings note that for the masculine endings the letters spell "loners."

There are, of course, exceptions to the above rules. For instance, **mano** *(hand)* is a feminine word even though it ends with the letter -o and **día** *(day)* is wa masculine word even though it ends with the letter -a. Your textbook and instructor will point out the exceptions that you will need to learn.

CAREFUL — Do not rely on biological gender to indicate the grammatical gender of Spanish equivalents of nouns that can refer to a man or a woman. For instance, the grammatical gender of the noun "**persona**" *(person)* is always feminine, even though the person being referred to could be a man or a woman.

WHAT IS MEANT BY NUMBER?

NUMBER in the grammatical sense means that a word can be   1
classified as singular or plural. When a word refers to one
person or thing, it is said to be SINGULAR; when it refers to
more than one, it is PLURAL.

> one *book*   two *books*
> | |
> singular   plural

More parts of speech indicate number in Spanish than in
English and there are also more spelling and pronunciation
changes in Spanish than in English.

ENGLISH	SPANISH	
nouns	nouns	10
verbs	verbs	
pronouns	pronouns	
demonstrative adjectives	adjectives	
	articles	

Since each part of speech follows its own rules to indicate
number, you will find number discussed in the sections
dealing with articles, the various types of adjectives and pronouns, as well as in all the sections on verbs. In this section
we shall only look at the number of nouns.   20

IN ENGLISH

A singular noun is made plural in one of two ways:

1. a singular noun can add an *"-s"* or *"-es"*

book	book*s*
church	church*es*

2. other singular nouns change their spelling

man	men
mouse	mice
leaf	leaves	30
child	children

Some nouns, called COLLECTIVE NOUNS, refer to a group of persons or things, but the noun itself is considered singular.

> A football *team* has eleven players.
> My *family* is well.

IN SPANISH

As in English, the plural form of a noun is usually spelled differently from the singular form.

1. The most common change is the same as the one made in English; that is, an "-s" is added to singular masculine or feminine nouns that end in a vowel.

	SINGULAR	PLURAL		
MASCULINE	libro	libros	*book*	*books*
FEMININE	mesa	mesas	*table*	*tables*

2. Nouns that end in a consonant add "-es" to form a plural.

	SINGULAR	PLURAL		
MASCULINE	papel	papeles	*paper*	*papers*
FEMININE	ciudad	ciudades	*city*	*cities*

A few nouns will have internal spelling changes when they become plural. Your instructor and textbook will point out the exceptions to the two basic rules listed above.

As in English, collective nouns in Spanish refer to a group of persons or things, but the noun itself is considered singular. Here are some common examples:

la banda	*band*
el equipo	*team*
la familia	*family*

WHAT ARE ARTICLES?

An ARTICLE is a word placed before a noun to show whether the noun refers to a specific person, animal, place, thing, event, or idea, or whether it refers to a non-specific person, thing, or idea.

> I saw *the* boy you spoke about.
> a specific boy

> I saw *a* boy in the street.
> not a specific boy

In English and in Spanish there are two types of articles: DEFINITE ARTICLES and INDEFINITE ARTICLES.

DEFINITE ARTICLES
IN ENGLISH

A DEFINITE ARTICLE is used before a noun when referring to a specific person, place, animal, thing, or idea. There is one definite article: ***the***.

> I read *the* book you recommended.
> a specific book

> I ate *the* apple you gave me.
> a specific apple

The definite article remains *the* when the noun that follows becomes plural.

> I read *the books* you recommended.
> I ate *the apples* you gave me.

IN SPANISH

As in English, a definite article is used before a noun when referring to a specific person, place, animal, thing, or idea.

> Comí **la** manzana que me diste.
> *I ate **the** apple you gave me.*

In Spanish, the article works hand-in-hand with the noun to which it belongs in that it matches the noun's gender and number. This "matching" is called AGREEMENT. One says that "the article *agrees* with the noun." (See *What is Meant by Gender?*, p. 12 and *What is Meant by Number?*, p. 15.)

Consequently, a different article is used depending on whether the noun is masculine or feminine (gender) and depending on whether the noun is singular or plural (number).

There are four forms of the definite article: two singular forms and two plural forms.

- **el** indicates that the noun is masculine singular

el libro	*the book*
el muchacho	*the boy*

- **la** indicates that the noun is feminine singular

la casa	*the house*
la muchacha	*the girl*

- **los** indicates that the noun is masculine plural

los libros	*the books*
los muchachos	*the boys*

- **las** indicates that the noun is feminine plural

las casas	*the houses*
las muchachas	*the girls*

Memorize nouns with the singular definite article; in most cases the article will tell you if the noun is masculine or feminine.[1]

CAREFUL — Unlike English where nouns are sometimes used without a preceding article, Spanish nouns are preceded by an article.

Me gustan **los gatos** pero odio **los perros**.
*I like **cats** [in general] but I hate **dogs** [in general].*

El español es un idioma bonito.
***Spanish** is a beautiful language.*

INDEFINITE ARTICLES
IN ENGLISH

An **INDEFINITE ARTICLE** is used before a noun when we are not speaking about a specific person, animal, place, thing, event, or idea. There are two indefinite articles: *a* and *an*.

---

[1]There are only a few exceptions to this statement. The primary exceptions are those feminine nouns that begin with a stressed a- and which for pronunciation purposes take **el** as the article: **el agua, el águila**. The noun is nonetheless feminine: **el agua fría**.

- *a* is used before a word beginning with a consonant[1]

    I saw *a* boy in the street.

    not a specific boy

- *an* is used before a word beginning with a vowel

    I ate *an* apple.

    not a specific apple

The indefinite article is used only with a singular noun. To indicate a nonspecific plural noun, the word *some* can be used, but it is usually left out.

    I saw boys in the street.
    I saw *(some)* boys in the street.

    I ate apples.
    I ate *(some)* apples.

IN SPANISH

As in English, an indefinite article is used before a noun when we are not speaking about a specific person, animal, place, thing, event, or idea.

Just as with definite articles, indefinite articles must agree with the noun's gender and number.

There are four forms of the indefinite article: two singular forms and two plural forms.

- **un** indicates that the noun is masculine singular

    un libro   *a book*
    un muchacho   *a boy*

- **una** indicates that the noun is feminine singular

    una casa   *a house*
    una muchacha   *a girl*

- **unos** indicates that the noun is masculine plural

    unos libros   *(some)* books
    unos muchachos   *(some) boys*

- **unas** indicates that the noun is feminine plural

    unas casas   *(some) houses*
    unas muchachas   *(some) girls*

Your textbook will instruct you on additional uses of the definite and indefinite articles in Spanish.

---

[1]Vowels are the sounds associated with the letters *a, e, i, o, u* and sometimes *y*; consonants are the sounds associated with the other letters of the alphabet.

Flashcards (see *Tips for Learning Vocabulary*, pp. 2-5)

1. Make a flashcard for each new noun. On the Spanish side, list the singular form; list the plural form only if it is irregular.

2. Use blue cards or blue ink/font for masculine nouns and red cards or red ink/font for feminine nouns.

3. Precede the noun with the appropriate definite article: **el** or **la**.

Pattern

1. Memorize the noun endings that indicate gender (see p. 14). Make sure that you memorize a sample word for each ending.

2. As you learn a new noun, look at its ending to see if the above list applies. If it does, the noun's gender will be easier to remember.

Practice

1. Whether you're looking at the Spanish or the English side of the card, as you say the Spanish noun and article, add a word such as "nuevo" (*new*) whose ending changes according to whether it accompanies a masculine or feminine noun (with a masculine noun the form is **nuevo**; with a feminine noun the form is **nueva**). The change in the form of the word will help reinforce the noun's gender in your memory.

el libro (nuev**o**)	*the (new) book*
la casa (nuev**a**)	*the (new) house*

2. Don't forget that it is only by practice and repeated use that you will remember the words and their gender.

CHAPTER

WHAT IS THE POSSESSIVE?

The term **POSSESSIVE** means that one noun owns or *possesses* another noun.

Mary's Spanish book is on the table.
| possessor | item possessed |

IN ENGLISH

There are two constructions to show possession.

1. An apostrophe can be used. In this construction, the possessor comes before the item possessed.

   - singular possessor adds an apostrophe + "s"

     Mary's dress
     a tree's branches
     singular possessor

   - plural possessor ending with "s" adds an apostrophe after the "s"

     the students' teacher
     the girls' club
     plural possessor

   - plural possessor not ending with "s" adds an apostrophe + "s"

     the children's playground
     the men's department
     plural possessor

2. The word *of* can be used. In this structure, the item possessed comes before the possessor.

   - a singular or plural possessor is preceded by *of the* or *of a*

     the book *of the* professor
     the branches *of a* tree
     singular possessor

     the teacher *of the* students
     plural possessor

IN SPANISH

There is only one way to express possession and that is by using the "of" construction (No. 2 above). The apostrophe structure (No. 1 above) does not exist.

The Spanish structure parallels the English structure using the word "of": item or noun possessed + **de** (*of*) + definite or indefinite article + the common noun possessor.

the professor's book	el libro **del** profesor
	de + el
	the book of the professor
the woman's purse	la bolsa **de la** señora
	the purse of the woman
a tree's branches	las ramas **de un** árbol
	the branches of a tree
the girls' father	el padre **de las** muchachas
	the father of the girls
the boys' team	el equipo **de los** muchachos
	the team of the boys

As in English, when the noun possessor is a proper noun, the definite or indefinite article is not used: item or noun possessed + **de** (*of*) + proper noun possessor.

Mary's dress	el vestido **de** María
possessor item possessed	item possessed possessor
	the dress of Mary

7

WHAT IS A VERB?

A **VERB** is a word that indicates a physical or mental action, a   1
condition, or an event. The verb is the basic element around
which a sentence is constructed.

Let us look at different types of words that are verbs:

- a physical action   to run, to hit, to talk, to walk
- a mental action   to hope, to believe, to imagine,
  to dream, to think
- a condition   to be, to feel, to have, to seem
- an event   to happen, to begin, to develop

Some verbs, however, do not seem to fall neatly into one of   10
the above categories. They are verbs nevertheless because
they represent the "core" of the sentence.

The book *costs* only $5.00.
|
to cost

The party *ended* at midnight.
|
to end

The verb is the most important word in a sentence. You
cannot write a **COMPLETE SENTENCE**, that is, express a complete
thought, without a verb.   20

   It is important to identify verbs because the function of the
other words in a sentence often depends on their relationship to the verb. For instance, the subject of a sentence is the
word doing the action of the verb and the object is the word
receiving the action of the verb (see *What is a Subject?*, p. 28,
and *What are Objects?*, p. 138).

IN ENGLISH

   To help you learn to recognize verbs, look at the paragraph below where the verbs are in italics.   30

   The three students *entered* the restaurant, *selected* a
   table, *hung* up their coats, and *sat* down. They *looked*
   at the menu and *asked* the waitress what she *recommended*. She *advised* the daily special. It *was* not
   expensive. They *chose* a bottle of red wine and *ordered*
   a salad. The service *was* slow, but the food *tasted* very
   good. Good cooking, they *decided, takes* time. They
   ate pastry for dessert and *finished* the meal with
   coffee.

IN SPANISH

40   Verbs are identified the same way as they are in English.

TERMS TO TALK ABOUT VERBS

- **INFINITIVE** OR **DICTIONARY FORM** — The verb form that is the name of the verb is called an infinitive: *to eat, to sleep, to drink* (see *What is the Infinitive?*, p. 25). In the dictionary a verb is listed without the "to": *eat, sleep, drink*.

- **CONJUGATION** — A verb is conjugated or changes in form to agree with its subject: *I do, he does* (see *What is a Verb Conjugation?*, p. 39).

50 - **TENSE** — A verb indicates tense, that is, the time (present, past, or future) of the action: *I am, I was, I will be* (see *What is Meant by Tense?*, p. 61).

- **MOOD** — A verb shows mood, that is, the speaker's attitude toward what he or she is saying (see *What is Meant by Mood?*, p. 86).

- **VOICE** — A verb shows voice, that is, the relation between the subject and the action of the verb (see *What is Meant by Active and Passive Voice?*, p. 103).

60 - **PARTICIPLE** — A verb may be used to form a participle: *writing, written; singing, sung* (see *What is a Participle?*, p. 73).

- **TRANSITIVE** OR **INTRANSITIVE** — A verb can be classified as transitive or intransitive depending on whether or not the verb can take a direct object (see pp. 138-9 in *What are Objects?*).

STUDY TIPS — VERB CONJUGATIONS (SEE P. 46)

WHAT IS THE INFINITIVE?

The **INFINITIVE** form is the name of the verb. The Spanish
equivalent of the infinitive *to study* is **estudiar**.

1

IN ENGLISH

The infinitive is composed of two words: *to* + the **DICTIO-
NARY FORM** of the verb *(to speak, to dance)*.

Although the infinitive is the most basic form of the
verb, it can never be used in a sentence without another
verb that is conjugated (see *What is a Verb Conjugation?*,
p. 39).

> *To learn* is exciting.
> infinitive conjugated verb

10

> It *is* important *to be* on time.
> conjugated verb infinitive

> Paul and Mary *want to dance* together.
> conjugated verb infinitive

The dictionary form of the verb, rather than the infinitive,
is used after such verbs as *let, must, should,* and *can.*

> Mr. Smith *let* his daughter *drive* his new car.
> dictionary form

20

> Paul *must be* home by noon.
> dictionary form

IN SPANISH

The infinitive form is composed of only one word. The
word "to" that is part of the English infinitive has no
Spanish equivalent. The Spanish infinitive is identified by
the last two letters of the verb called **THE ENDING**.

30

habl**ar**	*to speak*
com**er**	*to eat*
viv**ir**	*to live*

The infinitive form is important not only because it is the
form under which a verb is listed in the dictionary, but
also because the ending indicates the pattern that the verb
will follow to create its various forms.

40

1ˢᵀ CONJUGATION — verbs ending in -**ar** follow one pattern
2ᴺᴰ CONJUGATION — verbs ending in -**er** follow another pattern
3ᴿᴰ CONJUGATION — verbs ending in -**ir** follow another pattern

In a sentence the infinitive form is always used for a verb that follows any verb other than **ser** *(to be)*, **estar** *(to be)*, or **haber** *(to have)*.

*John and Mary want **to dance** together.*
Juan y María quieren **bailar** juntos.
|
infinitive

*I can **leave** tomorrow.*
Puedo **salir** mañana.
|
50 infinitive

*You should **study** more.*
Usted debe **estudiar** más.
|
infinitive

Notice that in the last two examples there is no "to" in the English sentence to alert you that an infinitive must be used in Spanish.

CAREFUL — You cannot depend upon the English sentence to alert you to the use of the infinitive in Spanish. Often the
60 word "to" will not be used in the English sentence but the infinitive must be used in Spanish.

CONSULTING THE DICTIONARY

In English it is possible to change the meaning of a verb by placing short words (prepositions or adverbs) after it.

For example, the verb *look* in Column A below changes meaning depending on the word that follows it *(to, after, for, into)*. In Spanish it is not possible to change the meaning of a verb by adding a preposition or an adverb as
70 in Column A. An entirely different Spanish verb corresponds to each meaning.

COLUMN A	MEANING	SPANISH
to look	→ to look at	**mirar**
	I *looked at* the photo.	
to look for	→ to search for	**buscar**
	I *am looking for* my book.	
to look after	→ to take care of	**cuidar**
	I *am looking after* the children.	
to look into	→ to study	**estudiar**
80 | | We*'ll look into* the problem. | |

When consulting an English-Spanish dictionary, all the examples above under Column A can be found under the dictionary entry *look* (**mirar**); however, you will have to search under that entry for the specific expression *look for* (**buscar**) or *look after* (**cuidar**) to find the correct Spanish equivalent.

Do not select the first entry under *look* and then add on the Spanish equivalent for *after, for, into,* etc.; the result will be meaningless in Spanish.

90

STUDY TIPS — VERBS

Flashcards (see *Tips for Learning Vocabulary,* pp. 2-5)

1. Use the digital flashcards that come with your textbook or create flashcards indicating the infinitive form of the Spanish verb on one side and its English equivalent on the other.

   aprender *to learn*

   You might want to select a particular color for verb cards so that later when you add information on the cards you can easily sort them out from the other cards (see *Study Tips — Verb Conjugations,* p. 46; *Tenses,* p. 63; *The Preterite,* p. 68; *The Future Tense,* p. 80).

2. If the verb is a reflexive verb, indicate "**se**" at the end of the infinitive (see *What are Reflexive Pronouns and Verbs?,* p. 159). If the verb can be used as a reflexive verb and as a non-reflexive verb, write both forms with examples.

   poner to put
   Juan **pone** los libros en su mochila. *John **puts** the books in his backpack.*

   ponerse to put on
   Juan **se pone** los zapatos. *John **puts on** his shoes.*

3. If the verb is followed by a preposition such as "de" or can be part of a special construction, indicate it on the card with an example.

   salir **de** *to leave*
   Salimos de la casa a las ocho. ***We leave** the house at eight.*

   tener (**que** + infinitive) *to have to + do something*
   Tenemos que estudiar mucho. ***We have to** study a lot.*

Practice

To learn the Spanish equivalent of English verbs follow the *Tips for Learning Vocabulary.* The real practice will come when you have learned to conjugate the verb and to use the conjugated forms in a sentence.

CHAPTER

9

WHAT IS A SUBJECT?

In a sentence the person or thing that performs the action of the verb is called the SUBJECT.

To find the subject of a sentence, always look for the verb first; then ask, *who?* or *what?* before the verb (see *What is a Verb?*, p. 23). The answer will be the subject.[1]

> Teresa speaks Spanish.
> VERB: speaks
> Who speaks Spanish? ANSWER: Teresa.
> The subject refers to one person; it is singular (see p. 15).

> Teresa's books cost a lot of money.
> VERB: cost
> What costs a lot of money? ANSWER: books.
> The subject refers to more than one thing; it is plural (p. 15).

■ If a verb has more than one subject, the subject is considered plural.

> The book and the pencil are on the table.
> VERB: are
> What is on the table? ANSWER: the book and the pencil.
> The subject refers to more than one thing; it is plural.

■ If a sentence has more than one verb, you have to find the subject of each verb.

> The boys were cooking while Mary set the table.
> *Boys* is the plural subject of *were*.
> *Mary* is the singular subject of *set*.

IN ENGLISH

Always ask *who?* or *what?* before the verb to find the subject. Never assume that the first word in the sentence is the subject. Subjects can be located in several different places, as you can see in the following examples (the subject is in **boldface** and the verb is *italicized*):

> *Did* **the game** *start* on time?
> After playing for two hours, **Paul** *became* exhausted.
> Mary's **brothers** *arrived* yesterday.

---

[1]The subject performs the action in an active sentence, but is acted upon in a passive sentence (see *What is Meant by Active and Passive Voice?*, p. 103).

IN SPANISH

The subject of a sentence is identified the same way as it is in English. Also, as in English, it can be located in different places in the sentence.

CAREFUL — In both English and Spanish it is important to find the subject of each verb to make sure that the verb form agrees with the subject (see *What is a Verb Conjugation?*, p. 39).

40

WHAT IS A PRONOUN?

A **PRONOUN** is a word used in place of one or more nouns. It may stand, therefore, for a person, animal, place, thing, event, or idea.

For instance, rather than repeating the proper noun "Paul" in the following sentences, "Paul" can be replaced by a pronoun in the second sentence.

Paul likes to swim. Paul practices every day.
Paul likes to swim. *He* practices every day.

A pronoun can only be used to refer to someone (or something) that has already been mentioned. The word that the pronoun replaces or refers to is called the **ANTECEDENT** of the pronoun. In the example above, the pronoun *he* refers to the proper noun *Paul*. *Paul* is the antecedent of the pronoun *he*.

There are different types of pronouns, each serves a different function and follows different rules. Listed below are the more important types and the chapters in which they are discussed.

PERSONAL PRONOUNS — These pronouns replace nouns referring to persons or things that have been previously mentioned. A different set of pronouns is often used depending on the pronoun's function in the sentence.

- subject (see p. 32)

    I go; *they* read; *he* runs; *she* sings.

- direct object pronouns (see p. 144)

    John loves *her*. Jane saw *him* at the theater.

- indirect object pronouns (see p. 148)

    John gave *us* the book. My mother wrote *me* a letter.

- object of preposition pronouns (p. 154)

    Robert is going to the movies with *us*.

REFLEXIVE PRONOUNS — These pronouns refer back to the subject of the sentence (see p. 159).

    I cut *myself.* We washed *ourselves.* Mary dressed *herself.*

INTERROGATIVE PRONOUNS — These pronouns are used to ask questions (see p. 169). (see p. 169)

> *Who* is that? *What* do you want?

DEMONSTRATIVE PRONOUNS — These pronouns are used to point out persons or things (see p. 177). (see p. 177)

> *This (one)* is expensive. *That (one)* is cheap.

POSSESSIVE PRONOUNS — These pronouns are used to show possession or ownership (see p. 163). (see p. 163)

> Whose book is that? *Mine. Yours* is on the table.

RELATIVE PRONOUNS — These pronouns are used to introduce relative subordinate clauses (see p. 180). (see p. 180)

> The man *who* just walked in is my instructor.
> This is the sweater *that* I bought last week.

INDEFINITE PRONOUNS — These pronouns are used to refer to unidentified persons or things.

> *One* should not do that.
> *Something* is wrong.

Spanish indefinite pronouns correspond in usage to their English equivalents. They can be studied in your textbook.

IN ENGLISH

Each type of pronoun follows a different set of rules.

IN SPANISH

As in English, each type of pronoun follows a different set of rules. In addition, Spanish pronouns usually correspond in gender and number with their antecedent.

CHAPTER

WHAT IS A SUBJECT PRONOUN?

A **SUBJECT PRONOUN** is a pronoun used as a subject of a verb.

> *He* worked while *she* read.
>> Who worked? ANSWER: He.
>> *He* is the subject of the verb *worked*.
>>
>> Who read? ANSWER: She.
>> *She* is the subject of the verb *read*.

Subject pronouns are divided into three groups: 1ˢᵗ, 2ⁿᵈ, and 3ʳᵈ person pronouns. The word **PERSON** in this instance does not necessarily mean a human being. It is a grammatical term that can refer to any noun.

IN ENGLISH

Here is a list of subject pronouns.

1ˢᵀ PERSON

I → the person speaking → SINGULAR
we → the person speaking plus others → PLURAL

> *Mary and I* are free this evening. *We* are going out.

2ⁿᴰ PERSON

you → the person or persons spoken to → SINGULAR or PLURAL

> *Paul*, do *you* like to sing?
> *Paul and Mary*, do *you* like to sing?

3ʳᴰ PERSON

he, she, it → the person or object spoken about → SINGULAR
they → the persons or objects spoken about → PLURAL

> *Mary and Paul* are free this evening. *They* are going out.

IN SPANISH

Spanish subject pronouns are also identified as 1ˢᵗ, 2ⁿᵈ and 3ʳᵈ persons. They are usually divided into singular and plural and presented in the following order.

SINGULAR		
1ˢᵀ PERSON	I	yo
2ⁿᴰ PERSON	you	tú
	he	él
3ʳᴰ PERSON	she	ella
	you	usted

PLURAL

1ST PERSON	we	{ nosotros nosotras
2ND PERSON	you	{ vosotros vosotras
3RD PERSON	{ they {	ellos ellas
	you	ustedes

As you can see above, there are three English subject pronouns that have more than one equivalent in Spanish: *you* (**tú, usted, vosotros, vosotras,** or **ustedes**), *we* (**nosotros** or **nosotras**), and *they* (**ellos** or **ellas**). Also there is one English subject pronoun, *it*, that has no equivalent in Spanish because *it* is generally not expressed.

Although *you* is a 2nd person pronoun since *you* is the person spoken to, two of its forms, **usted** and **ustedes**, are listed with 3rd person pronouns because they use the same forms as other 3rd person pronouns.

Let us look at the English subject pronouns that are either not expressed in Spanish *(it)*, or that have more than one Spanish equivalent *(you, we* and *they)*.

"YOU" (2nd PERSON SINGULAR AND PLURAL)

IN ENGLISH

The same pronoun "you" is used to address:

- any person or pet

  Do *you* have any questions, Mr. President?
  You are a good dog, Max.

- one or more persons

  Mary, are *you* coming with me?
  Mary and Paul, are *you* coming with me?

IN SPANISH

There are several words for "you" in Spanish. **Tú, vosotros** and **vosotras** are called the FAMILIAR FORM or the FAMILIAR "YOU." **Usted** and **ustedes** are called the FORMAL FORM or the FORMAL "YOU."

FAMILIAR "YOU" → TÚ, VOSOTROS OR VOSOTRAS

The familiar forms of "you" are used to address members of one's family (notice that the word "familiar" is similar to the word "family"), persons you call by their first name, children, and pets.

1. to address one person → **tú** (2nd person singular)

> *Mary, how are you?*
>> |
>> tú

> *John, how are you?*
>> |
>> tú

2. to address more than one person → **vosotros** or **vosotras** (2nd person plural)

- to address a group of two or more males → **vosotros**

> *John and Paul, how are you?*
>> masc. pl.   vosotros (masc. pl.)

- to address a group of two or more females → **vosotras**

> *Mary and Gloria, how are you?*
>> fem. pl.   vosotras (fem. pl.)

- to address a group of males and females → **vosotros**

> *John, Gloria and Mary, how are you?*
>> masc.   fem.   fem.   vosotros (masc. pl.)

The familiar plural forms **vosotros** and **vosotras** are used only in Spain. In Latin America **ustedes** is used as the plural of **tú** (see below).

FORMAL "YOU" → USTED OR USTEDES
The formal forms of "you" are used to address persons you do not know well enough to call by a first name or to whom you should show respect (Ms. Smith, Mr. Jones, Dr. Anderson, Professor Gómez).

1. to address one person → **usted** (singular)

> *Mr. García, how are you?*
>> |
>> usted

> *Mrs. García, how are you?*
>> |
>> usted

2. to address a group of males or females → **ustedes** (plural)

> *Professor Gómez and Mrs. García, how are you?*
>> masc. sing.   fem. sing.   ustedes

In Latin America **ustedes** is the plural of both the familiar and formal forms.

CAREFUL — If in doubt as to whether to use the familiar or formal forms when addressing an adult, use the formal forms. They show respect for the person you are talking to and use of familiar forms might be considered rude.

CHOOSING THE PROPER FORM OF "YOU"
In order to choose the correct form of "you" in Spanish, you should go through the following steps:

1. Determine whether the familiar or formal form is appropriate.   130
2. If the familiar form is appropriate, determine how many persons are being addressed:
   A. one person → **tú**

   B. more than one person:

   ▪ IN LATIN AMERICA → **ustedes**

   ▪ IN SPAIN → determine the gender of the persons being addressed:
      a) a group of males or males and females → **vosotros**   140
      b) a group of females → **vosotras**

3. If the formal form is appropriate, determine how many persons are being addressed:
   A. one person → **usted**

   B. more than one person → **ustedes**

Here is a chart you can use as a reference.

		ENGLISH	SPANISH	
			SPAIN	LATIN AMERICA
FAMILIAR	SINGULAR	*you*	tú	tú
	PLURAL	*you*	vosotros vosotras	ustedes
FORMAL	SINGULAR	*you*	usted	usted
	PLURAL	*you*	ustedes	ustedes

150

Let's find the Spanish equivalent for *you* in the following sentences:

*John, are **you** coming with us?*   160
    FAMILIAR OR FORMAL: familiar
    SINGULAR OR PLURAL: singular *(John)*
    SELECTION: **tú**
Juan, ¿vienes **tú** con nosotros?

*Isabel and Gloria, are **you** coming with us?*
Familiar or formal: familiar
Singular or plural: plural *(Isabel, Gloria)*
Spain or Latin America: Spain
Males, females or mixed group: females
Selection: **vosotras**

Isabel y Gloria, ¿venís **vosotras** con nosotros?

170

*Vincent and John, are **you** coming with us?*
Familiar or formal: familiar
Singular or plural: plural *(Vincent, John)*
Spain or Latin America: Latin America
Selection: **ustedes**

Vicente y Juan, ¿vienen **ustedes** con nosotros?

*Mr. President, are **you** coming with us?*
Familiar or formal: formal
Singular or plural: singular *(Mr. President)*
Selection: **usted**

180

Señor Presidente, ¿viene **usted** con nosotros?

*Mr. and Mrs. Lado, are **you** coming with us?*
Familiar or formal: formal
Singular or plural: plural *(Mr., Mrs. Lado)*
Selection: **ustedes**

Señor y señora Lado, ¿vienen **ustedes** con nosotros?

"IT" (3ᴿᴰ PERSON SINGULAR)

IN ENGLISH

190

Whenever you are speaking about one thing or idea, you use the subject pronoun "it."

Where is the book? *It* is on the table.
John has an idea. *It* is very interesting.

IN SPANISH

The subject pronoun "it" is not generally expressed.

¿Dónde está el libro? **Está** sobre la mesa.
It is understood as part of the verb **está**.
*Where is the book? **It is** on the table.*

200

"WE" (1ˢᵀ PERSON PLURAL)

IN ENGLISH

The subject pronoun "we" refers to the person speaking plus others.

John and I are going to the movies.
We are leaving at seven o'clock.

IN SPANISH

The subject pronoun used depends on the gender of the noun "we" replaces. In other words, the Spanish pronoun must agree with the gender of the antecedent.   210

- masculine antecedents → **nosotros**

> Juan y yo vamos al cine. **Nosotros** salimos a las siete.
>
> masc. masc. (man speaking) masc. pl.
> antecedents   pronoun
> *John and I are going to the movies.* ***We*** *are leaving at seven o'clock.*

- feminine antecedent → **nosotras**

> María y yo vamos al cine. **Nosotras** salimos a las siete.
>
> fem.   fem. (woman speaking) fem. pl.
> antecedents   pronoun
> *Mary and I are going to the movies.* ***We*** *are leaving at seven o'clock.*   220

- antecedents of different genders → **nosotros**

> Juan, María y yo vamos al cine. **Nosotros** salimos a las siete.
>
> masc. fem. masc. or fem.   masc. pl.
>   └ antecedents ┘   pronoun
> *John, Mary and I are going to the movies.* ***We*** *are leaving at seven o'clock.*

"THEY" (3ʳᴰ ᴘᴇʀsᴏɴ ᴘʟᴜʀᴀʟ)

IN ENGLISH

Whenever you are speaking about more than one person   230
or object, you use the subject pronoun "they."

> My brothers play tennis. *They* practice a lot.
> My sisters play soccer. *They* practice every day.
> Where are the books? *They* are on the table.

IN SPANISH

The subject pronoun used depends on the gender of the noun "they" replaces. In other words, the Spanish pronoun must agree with the gender of the antecedent.

- masculine antecedent → **ellos**   240

> Mis hermanos juegan al tenis. **Ellos** practican cada día.
>
> masc. pl.   masc. pl.
> antecedent   pronoun
> *My brothers play tennis.* ***They*** *practice every day.*

- feminine antecedent → **ellas**

> Mis hermanas juegan al fútbol. **Ellas** practican cada día.
>
> fem. pl.   fem. pl.
> antecedent   pronoun
> *My sisters play soccer.* ***They*** *practice every day.*   250

- antecedents of different genders → **ellos**

Juan, María y Gloria juegan al fútbol. **Ellos** practican cada día.
    | | | |
masc. fem.   fem.   masc. pl.
antecedents   pronoun
*John, Mary and Gloria play soccer. **They** practice every day.*

Just as the subject pronoun "it" is not expressed in Spanish, the subject pronoun "they" is not expressed when *they* refers to something other than people.

260

¿Dónde están los libros? **Están** sobre la mesa.
They is understood as part of the verb **están**.
*Where are the books? **They are** on the table.*

STUDY TIPS — SUBJECT PRONOUNS

Flashcards
Create a flashcard for each subject pronoun (1st, 2nd, and 3rd person singular and plural). You'll add the other forms of the pronoun when you learn them (see *Direct Object Pronouns*, pp. 145-6, *Indirect Object Pronouns*, pp. 149-51, and *Object of Preposition Pronouns*, pp. 154-5).

                    yo   *I*
                    ella   *she*

Practice
You'll practice subject pronouns when you practice conjugating verbs (see *Study Tips — Verb Conjugations*, p. 46).

WHAT IS A VERB CONJUGATION?

A **VERB CONJUGATION** is a list of the six possible forms of the verb for a particular tense. For each tense, there is one verb form for each of the six persons used as the subject of the verb.

> I am
> you are
> he, she, it is
> we are
> you are
> they are

Different tenses have different verb forms, but the principle of conjugation remains the same. In this chapter all our examples are in the present tense (see *What is the Present Tense?*, p. 64).

IN ENGLISH

The verb *to be* conjugated above is the English verb that changes the most; it has three forms: *am, are,* and *is.* (The initial vowel is often replaced by an apostrophe: *I'm, you're, he's.*) Other English verbs only have two forms such as the verb *to sing.*

SINGULAR

1ST PERSON	I *sing*
2ND PERSON	you *sing*
3RD PERSON	he *sings*
	she *sings*
	it *sings*

PLURAL

1ST PERSON	we *sing*
2ND PERSON	you *sing*
3RD PERSON	they *sing*

Because English verbs change so little, it isn't necessary to learn "to conjugate a verb;" that is, to list all its possible forms. For most verbs, it is much simpler to say that the verb adds an "-s" in the 3rd person singular.

IN SPANISH

Unlike English, Spanish verb forms change from one person to another so that when you learn a new verb, you must also learn how to conjugate it. First, you must establish whether the verb is regular or irregular.

- Verbs whose forms follow a predictable pattern are called REGULAR VERBS. Only one example must be memorized and the pattern can then be applied to other verbs in the same group (see p. 44).
- Verbs whose forms do not follow a predictable pattern are called IRREGULAR VERBS. The conjugation of these verbs must be memorized individually.

CHOOSING THE PROPER "PERSON" (see p. 32)

Below is the conjugation of the regular verb **cantar** *(to sing)*. Notice that each of the six persons has its own ending and that different subject pronouns belonging to the same person have the same verb form. Since the subject pronouns **usted** and **ustedes** use the verb form of the 3ʳᵈ person, they are listed with that person. Therefore, **él**, **ella** and **usted**, have the same verb form: **canta**.

SINGULAR

1ˢᵗ PERSON	yo canto	*I sing*
2ᴺᴰ PERSON	tú cantas	*you sing*
3ᴿᴰ PERSON	él canta	*he sings, it sings*
	ella canta	*she sings, it sings*
	usted canta	*you sing*

PLURAL

1ˢᵗ PERSON	nosotros cantamos	*we sing*[1]
	nosotras cantamos	*we sing*
2ᴺᴰ PERSON	vosotros cantáis	*you sing*
	vosotras cantáis	*you sing*
3ᴿᴰ PERSON	ellos cantan	*they sing*
	ellas cantan	*they sing*
	ustedes cantan	*you sing*

To choose the proper verb form, it is important to identify the person (1ˢᵗ, 2ⁿᵈ or 3ʳᵈ) and the number (singular or plural) of the subject.

1ˢᵗ PERSON SINGULAR — The subject is always **yo** *(I)*.

Generalmente **yo canto** bien.
Generally I sing well.

Notice that **yo** is not capitalized except when it is the first word of a sentence.

---

[1]Many textbooks only list **nosotros** and **vosotros**. The same verb form applies to **nosotras** and **vosotras**.

2ᴺᴰ PERSON SINGULAR — The subject is always **tú** *(you).*

> Juan, **tú cantas** muy bien.
> *John, **you sing** very well.*

3ᴿᴰ PERSON SINGULAR — The subject can be expressed in one of four ways:

1. the 3ʳᵈ person singular masculine pronoun **él** *(he)* and the 3ʳᵈ person singular feminine pronoun **ella** *(she)*

> Generalmente **él canta** muy bien.
> *Generally **he sings** very well.*

> Generalmente **ella canta** muy bien.
> *Generally **she sings** very well.*

2. the singular pronoun **usted** *(you)*

> Señor Gómez, **usted canta** muy bien.
> *Mr. Gómez, **you sing** very well.*

> Señorita Gómez, **usted canta** muy bien.
> *Miss Gómez, **you sing** very well.*

The pronoun **usted** is generally abbreviated as **Ud.** The abbreviation is used far more frequently than the entire word.

3. a proper noun

> María **canta** muy bien.
> *Mary **sings** very well.*

> Pedro **canta** muy bien.
> *Peter **sings** very well.*

> El señor García **canta** muy bien.
> *Mr. Garcia **sings** very well.*

>> In these three sentences the proper noun could be replaced by the pronoun *she* (**ella** fem.) or *he* (**él** masc.) so that you must use the 3ʳᵈ person singular form of the verb.

4. a singular common noun

> El hombre **canta** muy bien.
> *The man **sings** very well.*

> La niña **canta** muy bien.
> *The girl **sings** very well.*

>> In these two sentences the common noun could be replaced by the pronoun *she* (**ella** fem.) or *he* (**él** masc.) so that you must use the 3ʳᵈ person singular form of the verb.

Remember that the subject pronoun "it" has no Spanish equivalent. It is generally not expressed but rather it is understood as part of the verb. (See *What is a Subject Pronoun?*, p. 32.)

> Juan y María tienen un pájaro. **Canta** muy bien.
> *John and Mary have a bird. **It sings** very well.*

1ˢᵀ PERSON PLURAL — The subject can be expressed in one of two ways:

1. the first person plural pronoun **nosotros** or **nosotras** *(we)*

> **Nosotros cantamos** bien.
> *We sing well.*

2. a multiple subject in which the speaker is included

> **Miguel, Gloria y yo cantamos** muy bien.
>   nosotros
>
> *Michael, Gloria and I sing very well.*

> The subjects *Michael, Gloria and I* could be replaced by the pronoun *we*, so that you must use the 1ˢᵗ person plural form of the verb.

2ᴺᴰ PERSON PLURAL — The subject can be expressed in one of two ways:

1. the second person plural pronoun **vosotros** or **vosotras** *(you)*

> **Vosotras cantáis** bien.
> *You sing well.*

2. a multiple subject in which the speaker is not included

> **Juan y tú cantáis** muy bien.
> *John and you sing very well.*

> In this sentence *John* (whom you would address with the **tú** form) and *you* (whom you also address with the **tú** form) could be replaced by the pronoun *you*, so that you must use the 2ⁿᵈ person plural form of the verb.

The familiar plural "you form" of the verb (the **vosotros** form) is used only in Spain when you are speaking to two or more persons with whom you would use **tú** individually. Many beginning Spanish textbooks do not emphasize or practice the **vosotros** form. Your instructor will inform you if you need to learn the **vosotros** forms of verbs or not.

3ND PERSON PLURAL — The subject can be expressed in one of four ways: 160

1. the 3rd person plural masculine pronoun **ellos** *(they)* and the 3rd person plural feminine pronoun **ellas** *(they)*

> **Ellos cantan** muy bien.
> *They sing very well.*
>
> **Ellas cantan** muy bien.
> *They sing very well.*

2. the plural pronoun **ustedes** *(you)*

> Elena y Francisco, **ustedes cantan** muy bien.   170
> *Helen and Francis, you sing very well.*
>
>> In this sentence Helen (whom you would address with the **tú** form) and Francis (whom you also address with the **tú** form) could be replaced by the **ustedes** form of *you,* so that you must use the 3rd person plural form of the verb.

The pronoun **ustedes** is generally abbreviated as **Uds.** The abbreviation is used far more frequently than the entire word.

3. two or more proper or common nouns   180

> **Isabel, Gloria y Roberto cantan** muy bien.
> fem. + fem. + masc. (ellos)
> *Isabel, Gloria and Robert sing very well.*
>
> **La chica y su padre cantan** muy bien.
> fem. + masc. (ellos)
> *The girl and her father sing very well.*

4. a plural noun

> **Las chicas cantan** muy bien.
> fem. pl. (ellas)   190
> *The girls sing very well.*

Just as the subject pronoun "it" has no Spanish equivalent, "they" has no Spanish equivalent when it does not refer to persons.

> María tiene dos pájaros. **Cantan** muy bien.
> *Mary has two birds. **They sing** very well.*

HOW TO CONJUGATE A VERB

A Spanish verb, whether regular or irregular, is composed of two parts:

1. The STEM, also called the "root," is the part of the verb left after dropping the last two letters from the infinitive (see *What is the Infinitive?*, p. 25).

INFINITIVE	STEM
cantar	cant-
comer	com-
vivir	viv-

In regular verbs the stem usually remains the same throughout a conjugation. However, in certain verbs called STEM-CHANGING VERBS, the stem will change in a minor way. (Your textbook will identify these verbs.)

2. The ENDING is the letter or letters added to the stem. The ending will change for each person in the conjugation of regular and irregular verbs.

Regular verbs are divided into three GROUPS, also called CONJUGATIONS, identified by the infinitive ending of the verb.

-ar	-er	-ir
1st group	2nd group	3rd group

Each of the three verb groups has its own set of endings for each tense (see *What is Meant by Tense?*, p. 61). Memorizing the conjugation of one sample verb for each group enables you to conjugate all the other regular verbs belonging to that group.

As an example of the steps to follow to conjugate a regular verb, let us look at verbs of the 1st group (**-ar** verbs), that is, verbs like **hablar** *(to speak)* and **tomar** *(to take)* that follow the pattern of **cantar** *(to sing)* conjugated on p. 40.

1. Identify the group of the verb by its infinitive ending.

> **hablar**　→　**-ar** verbs or 1st conjugation or group
> **tomar**

2. Find the verb stem by removing the infinitive ending.

> habl-
> tom-

3. Add the ending that agrees with the subject.

yo	hablo	yo	tomo
tú	hablas	tú	tomas

él		él	
ella	} habla	ella	} toma
usted		usted	

nosotros	} hablamos	nosotros	} tomamos
nosotras		nosotras	

vosotros	} habláis	vosotros	} tomáis
vosotras		vosotras	

ellos		ellos	
ellas	} hablan	ellas	} toman
ustedes		ustedes	

The endings of regular verbs belonging to the other groups are different, but the process of conjugation is the same. Just follow the three steps above.

As irregular verbs are introduced in your textbook, their entire conjugation will be given. Be sure to memorize them because many common verbs are irregular (**tener**, *to have*; **ser**, *to be*; **ir**, *to go*; **hacer**, *to make*, for example).

OMITTING THE SUBJECT PRONOUN IN SPANISH

As you can see, the Spanish verb ending indicates the subject. For instance, **hablo** can only have **yo** *(I)* as a subject. When the verb ending can only refer to one subject, the subject pronoun is often omitted.

hablo	*I speak*
hablas	*you speak*
hablamos	*we speak*
habláis	*you speak*

However, since the verb ending of the 3rd person singular and plural forms can refer to several different persons, it is often necessary to include the pronoun.

habla could be	{	él habla	*he speaks*
	{	ella habla	*she speaks*
	{	Ud. habla	*you speak*
hablan could be	{	ellos hablan	*they speak*
	{	ellas hablan	*they speak*
	{	Uds. hablan	*you speak*

240

250

260

270

Pattern (see *Tips for Learning Word Forms,* pp. 3-4)

1. Start by looking for a pattern within the conjugation of the verb itself. Let's look at similarities between the various conjugations of regular verbs: **preguntar** *(to ask)*, **aprender** *(to learn)*, **vivir** *(to live)*.

INFINITIVE:		preguntar	aprender	vivir
STEM:		pregunt-	aprend-	viv-
1ˢᵗ per. sing.	(yo)	pregunto	aprendo	vivo
2ⁿᵈ per. sing.	(tú)	preguntas	aprendes	vives
3ʳᵈ per. sing.	(él, etc.)	pregunta	aprende	vive
1ˢᵗ per. pl.	(nosotros)	pregunt**amos**	aprend**emos**	viv**imos**
2ⁿᵈ per. pl.	(vosotros)	pregunt**áis**	aprend**éis**	viv**ís**
3ʳᵈ per. pl.	(ellos, etc.)	pregunt**an**	aprend**en**	viven

What pattern do you see?

- 1ˢᵗ pers. sing.: all end in -**o**
- 2ⁿᵈ pers. sing.: all end in -**s**, -**ar** and -**er** verbs add the -**s** after the vowel of the infinitive (-**a** and -**e**), but -**ir** verbs add the -**s** after the vowel -**e**
- 3ʳᵈ pers. sing.: -**ar** and -**er** verbs end with the vowel of the infinitive (-**a** and -**e**), but -**ir** verbs end with the vowel -**e** (same vowel as used for 2ⁿᵈ pers. sing.)
- 1ˢᵗ pers. pl.: all end with -**mos** after the vowel of the infinitive (-**a**, -**e** and -**i**)
- 2ⁿᵈ pers. pl.: all end in -**is** after the vowel of the infinitive on which there is an accent (-**á**, -**é** and -**í**)
- 3ʳᵈ pers. pl.: all end in -**n**, -**ar** and -**er** verbs add the -**n** after the vowel of the infinitive (-**a** and -**e**), but -**ir** verbs add the -**n** after the vowel -**e** (same vowel as used for 2ⁿᵈ and 3ʳᵈ pers. sing.)

2. Whenever you learn a new verb, look for similarities in the pattern with another verb. Here are two stem-changing verb patterns.

cont**ar** *(to count)*		pod**er** *(to be able to)*	
cuento	cont**amos**	**pued**o	pod**emos**
cuentas	cont**áis**	**pued**es	pod**éis**
cuenta	**cuent**an	**pued**e	**pued**en

pens**ar** *(to think)*		entend**er** *(to understand)*	
pienso	pens**amos**	**entiend**o	entend**emos**
piensas	pens**áis**	**entiend**es	entend**éis**
piensa	**piens**an	**entiend**e	**entiend**en

3. Even irregular verbs will have some type of pattern. For instance, make a list of the similarities between the conjugation of **dar** *(to give)*, **ir** *(to go)*, **ser** *(to be)*, **estar** *(to be)*.

		dar	**ir**	**ser**	**estar**
INFINITIVE:		dar	ir	ser	estar
1ˢᵗ per. sing.	(yo)	doy	voy	soy	estoy
2ⁿᵈ per. sing.	(tú)	das	vas	eres	estás
3ʳᵈ per. sing.	(él, etc.)	da	va	es	está
1ˢᵗ per. pl.	(nosotros)	damos	vamos	somos	estamos
2ⁿᵈ per. pl.	(vosotros)	dais	vais	sois	estáis
3ʳᵈ per. pl.	(ellos, etc.)	dan	van	son	están

What similarities did you see? Compare your list to the one below.

- 1ˢᵗ pers. sing.: all end in -**oy** (instead of –**o** like regular verbs)
- 2ⁿᵈ pers. sing.: all end in –**s** like regular verbs

- 1ˢᵗ pers. pl.: all end in **–mos** like regular verbs
- 3ʳᵈ pers. pl.: all end in **–n** like regular verbs
- the forms of **ir** and **dar** are alike except for the first letter
- **ir** and **dar** are conjugated as if they were regular **–ar** verbs, except for the 1ˢᵗ pers. sing. and accents

3. As new verb conjugations are introduced, more and more similarities and patterns will become evident. Take the time to look for them; it will make learning conjugations much easier and faster.

Flashcards (see also *Study Tips – Tenses*, p. 63).

To review verbs and their conjugations, use flashcards to learn the meaning of the verbs (see p. 27) and add the following information on the Spanish side:

1. Indicate if the verb is regular (reg.) or irregular (irreg.) so that you can review irregular verbs separately.

> bailar *(reg.)*   *to dance*
> hacer *(irreg.)*   *to do, to make*

2. If the verb is irregular but shares a pattern with another verb, indicate the other verb.

> merecer *(irreg.)*   *to deserve*
> *(like* conocer → *to know)*

3. If the verb is irregular only in one form, write down that it is regular except for that one form.

> salir *(irreg.)*   *to leave*
> (regular **-ir**, except **yo salgo**)

4. If the verb is a stem-changing verb, indicate its type (**ie, ue, i**) in parentheses (see your textbook for types of stem-changing verbs).

> pensar (**ie**)   *to think*
> volver (**ue**)   *to return*
> pedir (**i**)   *to ask for, to request*

Practice

1. As you learn the different forms of a verb, write them down as many times as you need to so that you are able to write them without using your textbook.
2. Practice using the various forms out of order, so that if you are asked a question you can respond without going through the entire conjugation in your head.
3. Apply the pattern you've just learned to another verb with the same conjugation, if there is one.
4. Be sure to do the exercises that follow the introduction of a new conjugation in your textbook and workbook. If you have to refer to your textbook, notes or flashcards to do the exercises, you haven't really learned the forms.
5. Create and write down your own sentences using the different forms of the verb, or preferably with other verbs that are conjugated the same way.

CHAPTER

WHAT ARE SENTENCES, CLAUSES, AND PHRASES?

WHAT IS A SENTENCE?

A SENTENCE is the expression of a thought usually consisting at least of a subject and a verb (see *What is a Subject?*, p. 28 and *What is a Verb?*, p. 23).

María studies.
subject verb

A sentence may also have a direct and an indirect object (see *What are Objects?*, p. 138).

María speaks Spanish.
subject verb direct object

María speaks Spanish to her parents.
subject verb direct object indirect object

In addition, a sentence may include various kinds of modifiers: adjectives (see *What is an Adjective?*, p. 108), adverbs (see *What is an Adverb?*, p. 130) and phrases (see below).

WHAT IS A CLAUSE?

A CLAUSE is a group of words in a sentence containing a subject and a conjugated verb which works as a unit of meaning. A clause can also include modifiers, such as adjectives and adverbs. There are two kinds of clauses: main and subordinate clauses.

- A MAIN CLAUSE, or INDEPENDENT CLAUSE, generally expresses a complete thought, the important idea of the sentence. If it were taken out of the sentence, it could stand alone as a complete sentence.

- A SUBORDINATE CLAUSE, or DEPENDENT CLAUSE, does not express a complete thought; it must be combined with a main clause. It can start with a subordinating conjunction (see pp. 132-3) or a relative pronoun (see p. 180). A subordinate clause starting with a subordinating conjunction can come at the beginning or at the end of a sentence.

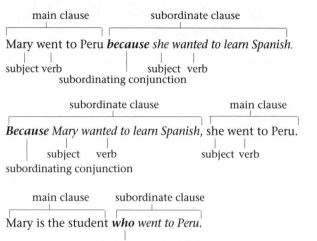

IN ENGLISH

There is no set position for the verb in a sentence or clause, but the subject usually comes before the verb.

IN SPANISH

As in English, there is no set position for the verb in a sentence or clause, but the subject usually comes before the verb.

WHAT IS A PHRASE?

A **PHRASE** is a sequence of two or more words, not including a subject or a conjugated verb, that functions as a unit of meaning in a sentence. The various phrases are identified by the **HEAD**, i.e., the part of speech of the essential word of the phrase. The other words in the phrase, called **MODIFIERS**, give additional information about the head.

- **NOUN PHRASE** — noun + modifier(s)

    María is *a conscientious **student***.

- **ADJECTIVE PHRASE** — adjective + modifier(s)

    María was ***wise** beyond her years*.

- **DEMONSTRATIVE PHRASE** — demonstrative pronoun + noun

    ***This** book* is mine; whose are ***those** books?*

- **PREPOSITIONAL PHRASE** — preposition + noun/pronoun object

    María fell asleep ***during** the lecture*.

▪ **VERB PHRASE** — verb + words to specify a particular meaning of the verb

María **looks** *after* the child. *[takes care of]*

PARTICIPIAL PHRASE — participle + objects + modifiers

The boys came **running** *at full speed.*

ADVERBIAL PHRASE — adverb + modifier(s)

María ran **very quickly.**

> adverbs

INFINITIVE PHRASE — infinitive (+ object) + modifier(s)

I don't want María **to go** *on a trip.*

TYPES OF SENTENCES: SIMPLE, COMPOUND, AND COMPLEX

WHAT IS A SIMPLE SENTENCE?

A **SIMPLE SENTENCE** consists of one main clause.

Mary liked the trip.
subject verb object

WHAT IS A COMPOUND SENTENCE?

A **COMPOUND SENTENCE** consists of two main clauses joined by a coordinating conjunction (see p. 132).

main clause 1   main clause 2

Mary liked Spain, but she found it expensive.
subject verb   subject verb
         coordinating
         conjunction

WHAT IS A COMPLEX SENTENCE?

A **COMPLEX SENTENCE** consists of a main clause and one or more subordinate clauses (see p. 48).

main clause   subordinate clause

Mary liked Mexico because the people are friendly.
subject verb   subordinating subject verb
                 conjunction

WHAT ARE AFFIRMATIVE AND
NEGATIVE SENTENCES?

A sentence can be classified according to whether or not the   1
verb is negated, that is, made negative with the word *not* or
another negative word such as *never, nobody,* or *nothing.*

An **AFFIRMATIVE SENTENCE** is a sentence whose verb is not
negated. It states a fact that is.

> Spain is a country in Europe.
> John will work in the university.
> They liked to travel.

A **NEGATIVE SENTENCE** is a sentence whose verb is negated with
a negative word such as *no, not, never.* It states that a fact or
situation is not true; it denies or negates the information it   10
contains.

> Spain is *not* a country in Latin America.
> John will *not* work in a factory.
> They *never* liked to travel.

IN ENGLISH

An affirmative sentence can be changed to a negative sentence in one of two ways:

1. by adding ***not*** after auxiliary words or auxiliary verbs (see
   What are Auxiliary Verbs?, p. 70)   20

AFFIRMATIVE	NEGATIVE
John *is* a student.	John is *not* a student.
Mary *can* do it.	Mary can*not* do it.
They *will* travel.	They will *not* travel.

   Frequently, the word *not* is attached to the verb and the
   letter "o" is replaced by an apostrophe; this is called a
   CONTRACTION: *is not* → *isn't; cannot* → *can't; will not* → *won't.*

2. by adding the auxiliary verb ***do, does***, or ***did*** + ***not*** + the
   dictionary form of the main verb. Note that *do* or *does* is
   used for negatives in the present tense and *did* for nega-   30
   tives in the past tense—see *What is the Present Tense?*,
   p. 64 and *What is the Past Tense?*, p. 66.

AFFIRMATIVE	NEGATIVE
We *study* a lot.	We *do not* study a lot.
Julia *writes* well.	Julia *does not* write well.
The plane *arrived.*	The plane *did not* arrive.

Frequently, *do, does,* or *did* is contracted with *not: do not* → *don't; does not* → *doesn't; did not* → *didn't.*

IN SPANISH

The basic rule for turning an affirmative sentence into a negative sentence is far simpler than in English. You merely place **no** in front of the conjugated verb.

AFFIRMATIVE	NEGATIVE
Estudiamos mucho.	No **estudiamos** mucho.
	conjugated verb
*We **study** a lot.*	*We **do not** study a lot.*
Julia **escribe** bien.	Julia **no** escribe bien.
	conjugated verb
*Julia **writes** well.*	*Julia **does not** write well.*
El avión **llegó**.	El avión **no** llegó.
	conjugated verb
*The plane **arrived**.*	*The plane **didn't** arrive.*

CAREFUL — Remember that there is no equivalent for the auxiliary words *do, does, did* in Spanish; do not try to include them in negative sentences.

NEGATIVE WORDS

In both English and Spanish there are negative words that can be added to an affirmative sentence.

IN ENGLISH

The most common negative words are: *nothing, nobody, no one, never.*

> I have *nothing* for you.
> He *never* arrives on time.
> When John is angry, he speaks to *no one (nobody)*.

IN SPANISH

The most common negative words are **nada** *(nothing),* **nadie** *(nobody, no one),* and **nunca** *(never).* Often the negative word is used with **no** in the same sentence.

> **No** tengo **nada** para ti.
> *I have **nothing** for you. (I **don't** have **anything** for you.)*

> **Nunca** llega a tiempo.
> *He **never** arrives on time.*

Cuando Juan está enojado, **no** le habla a **nadie**.   80
*When John is angry, he speaks to **no one (nobody)**.*

The position of the negative word can change according to its function in the sentence. (See *What are Indefinites and Negatives?*, p. 186.)

NEGATIVE ANSWERS

IN ENGLISH

When answering a question negatively in English, both *no* and *not* will often appear in the answer.

Do you live near the park? *No*, I do *not* live near the park.   90

IN SPANISH

Since both *no* and *not* have the Spanish equivalent **no**, the word **no** will appear twice in the negative answer to the above question in Spanish.

¿Vives cerca del parque? **No**, **no** vivo cerca del parque.
                                     no not
*Do you live near the park? **No**, I do **not** live near the park.*

CHAPTER

WHAT ARE DECLARATIVE AND INTERROGATIVE SENTENCES?

1   A sentence can be classified as to whether it is making a statement or asking a question. A **DECLARATIVE SENTENCE** is a sentence that makes a statement. An **INTERROGATIVE SENTENCE** is a sentence that asks a question.

> DECLARATIVE   Columbus discovered America in 1492.
> INTERROGATIVE   Did Columbus discover America in 1492?

In written language, an interrogative sentence always ends with a question mark.

10   **IN ENGLISH**
A declarative sentence can be changed to an interrogative sentence in one of two ways:

1. by adding the auxiliary verb *do, does,* or *did* before the subject and changing the main verb to the dictionary form of the verb. Note that *do* or *does* are used to introduce a question in the present tense and *did* to introduce a question in the past tense—see *What is the Present Tense?*, p.64 and *What is the Past Tense?*, p. 66).

20

DECLARATIVE SENTENCE	INTERROGATIVE SENTENCE
Philip *likes* sports cars.	*Does* Philip *like* sports cars?
present 3ʳᵈ pers. sing.	present 3ʳᵈ pers. sing. + dictionary form
Paul and Mary *sing* well.	*Do* Paul and Mary *sing* well?
present 3ʳᵈ pers. pl.	present 3ʳᵈ pers. pl. + dictionary form
Mark *went* to Mexico.	*Did* Mark *go* to Mexico?
past	past + dictionary form

30   2. by inverting the normal word order of subject + verb to verb + subject. This **INVERSION** process can only be used with auxiliary verbs (AV) or auxiliary words (AW). See *What are Auxiliary Verbs?*, p. 70.

DECLARATIVE SENTENCE	INTERROGATIVE SENTENCE
Paul is home.	*Is Paul* home?
subject + verb *to be*	verb *to be* + subject

You have received a letter.   *Have you received* a letter?

subject + AV + main verb   AV + subject + main verb

She will come tomorrow.   *Will she come* tomorrow?

subject + AW + main verb   AW + subject + main verb

IN SPANISH

A declarative sentence can be changed to an interrogative sentence by using the inversion process.

In a simple declarative sentence that consists of a subject + verb, the word order of the question is verb + subject.

DECLARATIVE SENTENCE	INTERROGATIVE SENTENCE
Juan estudia.	¿Estudia Juan?
subject verb	verb subject
John studies.	*Does John study?*
Los niños cantan.	¿Cantan los niños?
subject verb	verb subject
The children sing.	*Do the children sing?*

Notice that in written Spanish the question is signaled at both the beginning and end of the sentence. The punctuation mark at the beginning of the sentence looks like an upside-down question mark (¿); a question mark like the one in English is located at the end of the sentence (?).

TAG QUESTIONS

In both English and Spanish when you expect a yes-or-no answer, you can also transform a statement into a question by adding a short phrase at the end of the statement. This short phrase is called a **TAG** or **TAG QUESTION**.

IN ENGLISH

There are different tags, depending on the tense of the verb of the statement and whether the statement is affirmative or negative. For instance, affirmative statements take negative tags and negative statements take affirmative tags.

John and Mary *are* friends, *aren't they?*

affirmative statement   negative tag

John and Mary *aren't* friends, *are they?*

negative statement   affirmative tag

IN SPANISH

The words ¿no?, ¿verdad?, or ¿no es verdad? can be added to the end of an affirmative statement to form a tag question.

> Juan y María son amigos, ¿no?
> *John and Mary are friends, **aren't they?***

> Trabajas mucho, ¿verdad?
> *You work hard, **don't you?***

> Hoy es miércoles, ¿no es verdad?
> *Today is Wednesday, **isn't it?***

The word ¿verdad? is generally added to the end of a negative statement to form a tag question.

> Juan y María no son amigos, ¿verdad?
> *John and Mary aren't friends, **are they?***

WHAT ARE SOME EQUIVALENTS OF "TO BE"?

IN ENGLISH

The verb *to be* has the following forms in the present
tense: *I am; you are; he, she, it is; we are; you are; they are.* It
is used in a variety of ways:

- to tell time

    It *is* 4:00 o'clock.

- to discuss health

    John *isn't* very well.

- to describe traits and characteristics

    Mary *is* tall and blond.

- to tell ages

    I *am* twenty years old.

- to explain what there is or there are in specific places

    There *are* twenty-five students in the class.

IN SPANISH

There are various verbs used to express the English verb *to be:*

ENGLISH	SPANISH
	1. **ser** *(to be)*
to be	2. **estar** *(to be)*
	3. **tener** *(to have)*
there is, there are	4. **hay** (a form of *to have*)

Depending on what you want to say, you will have to use
one of these four verbs. Here are a few rules to help you
select the correct one:

1. TO BE → "SER"

Use a form of the verb **ser** when you are speaking about
the following:

- to tell time

    It is 4:00 o'clock.
    Son las cuatro.

- to show possession
  That car is John's.
  Ese coche **es** de Juan.

  This book is yours.
  Este libro **es** tuyo.

40

- to express nationality and origin
  Mary is Spanish; she is from Madrid.
  María **es** española; **es** de Madrid.

- with nouns to identify someone or something
  Mr. Robles is a lawyer.
  El señor Robles **es** abogado.

  That building is the library.
  Ese edificio **es** la biblioteca.

- with adjectives to describe traits or characteristics

50

  Mary is tall and blond.
  María **es** alta y rubia.

2. To be → "Estar"

Use a form of the verb **estar** when you are speaking about the following:

- to express location
  John and I are in the library.
  Juan y yo **estamos** en la biblioteca.

  The books are on the table.

60

  Los libros **están** sobre la mesa.

- to discuss health
  How are you?
  ¿Cómo **está** Ud.?

  Mary is fine but John is sick.
  María **está** bien pero Juan **está** enfermo.

- with adjectives that describe a condition

  I am tired and worried.

  adjectives of condition

70

  Estoy cansada y preocupada.

"Ser" vs. "estar"

As you can see above, when the verb *to be* is followed by an adjective, both **ser** and **estar** can be used. In order to select the appropriate verb, you will need to identify the type of adjective.

- adjectives that describe physical characteristics and personality traits → **ser**

My house is modern.
|
characteristic

Mi casa **es** moderna.

> **Ser** is used because the adjective *modern* distinguishes the house from others. It answers the question: Which house is yours? or What is your house like?

Mary is nice.
|
trait

María **es** simpática.

> **Ser** is used because the adjective *nice* distinguishes Mary from other persons. It answers the question: What kind of person is Mary?

- adjectives that describe a condition → **estar**

My house is dirty.
|
condition

Mi casa **está** sucia.

> **Estar** is used because *dirty* describes a condition, not a characteristic of the house. It answers the question: What condition is the house in?

Mary is tired.
|
condition

María **está** cansada.

> **Estar** is used because the adjective *tired* describes a condition, not a characteristic of Mary. It answers the question: What is Mary's condition?

In a question, a different type of information is being requested depending on whether **ser** or **estar** is used.

¿Cómo **es** María?

> Use of **ser** → What is Mary like? What are her traits?

¿Cómo **está** María?

> Use of **estar** → How is Mary? What is her condition? How is she feeling?

3. TO BE → "TENER" *(to have)*

Sometimes the English expression *to be* + adjective is expressed with the Spanish verb *to have* (**tener**) + noun. These idiomatic expressions using **tener** + noun must be memorized.

80

90

100

110

Here are a few examples:

*I **am** hungry.*
to be + adjective
Tengo hambre.
to have + noun [word-for-word: I have hunger]

*I **am** twenty years old.*
to be   +   adjective
Tengo veinte años.
to have   + noun [word-for-word: I have twenty years]

4. THERE IS, THERE ARE → "HAY"

The English expressions *there is* or *there are* are translated with the Spanish word **hay**. **Hay** is INVARIABLE; that is, it does not change form since it can be either singular or plural.

*There **is** a book on the table.*
singular noun
Hay un libro sobre la mesa.

*There **are** many books on the table.*
plural noun
Hay muchos libros sobre la mesa.

Do not confuse the expession **hay** with the verb **estar**. To avoid using the wrong verb, see if you can replace the "is" or "are" of the English sentence with "there is" or "there are." If you can, you must use **hay**; if you can't, then **está** or **están** must be used.

*On the table **is** a book.*
there is [you can say: On the table *there is* a book.]
hay (to show presence)

*The book **is** on the table.*
is [you can't say: the book *there is* on the table]
está (to show location)

*In the classroom **are** students.*
there are [you can say: In the classroom *there are* students.]
hay (to show presence)

*The chairs **are** in the classroom.*
are [you can't say: the chairs *there are* in the classroom]
están (to show location)

WHAT IS MEANT BY TENSE?

The **TENSE** of a verb indicates when the action of the verb takes place: at the present time, in the past, or in the future. The word *tense* comes from the same word as the Spanish word "tiempo," which means *time*.

I am studying	PRESENT
I studied	PAST
I will study	FUTURE

As you can see in the above examples, just by putting the verb in a different tense and without giving any additional information (such as "I am studying *now*," "I studied *yesterday*," "I will study *tomorrow*"), you can indicate when the action of the verb takes place.

Tenses may be classified according to the way they are formed. A **SIMPLE TENSE** consists of only one verb form (I *studied),* while a **COMPOUND TENSE** consists of one or more auxiliaries plus the main verb (I *am studying,* I *had been studying*).

In this section we will only consider tenses of the indicative mood (see *What is Meant by Mood?,* p. 86).

IN ENGLISH

Listed below are the main tenses of the indicative mood whose equivalents you will encounter in Spanish:

PRESENT

I study	PRESENT
I do study	PRESENT EMPHATIC
I am studying	PRESENT PROGRESSIVE

PAST

I studied	SIMPLE PAST
I did study	PAST EMPHATIC
I have studied	PRESENT PERFECT
I was studying	PAST PROGRESSIVE
I had studied	PAST PERFECT

FUTURE

I will study	FUTURE
I will have studied	FUTURE PERFECT

CONDITIONAL

I would study	CONDITIONAL
I would have studied	CONDITIONAL PERFECT

1

10

20

30

As you can see, there are only two simple tenses (present and simple past). All of the other tenses are compound tenses.

IN SPANISH

Listed below are the main tenses of the indicative mood that you will encounter in Spanish.

PRESENT

estudio	*I study, I do study*	PRESENT
	I am studying	
estoy estudiando	*I am studying*	PRESENT PROGRESSIVE

PAST

estudié	*I studied, I did study*	PRETERITE
estudiaba	*I used to study*	IMPERFECT
	I was studying	
estaba estudiando	*I was studying*	PAST PROGRESSIVE
he estudiado	*I have studied*	PRESENT PERFECT
había estudiado	*I had studied*	PAST PERFECT

FUTURE

estudiaré	*I will study*	FUTURE
habré estudiado	*I will have studied*	FUTURE PERFECT

CONDITIONAL[1]

estudiaría	*I would study*	CONDITIONAL
habría estudiado	*I would have studied*	CONDITIONAL PERFECT

As you can see, there are more simple tenses than in English (present, preterite, imperfect, future, and conditional). The compound tenses in Spanish are formed with the auxiliary verbs **estar** *(to be)* or **haber** *(to have)* + the main verb.

This handbook discusses the various tenses and their usage in separate chapters: *What is the Present Tense?*, p. 64; *What is the Past Tense?*, p. 66; *What is the Future Tense?*, p. 78; *What is the Conditional?*, p. 98; *What are Progressive Tenses?*, p. 76; *What are Perfect Tenses?*, p. 82. Verb tenses can be grouped according to the mood in which they are used (see *What is Meant by Mood?*, p. 86).

CAREFUL — Do not assume that tenses with the same name are used in the same way in English and in Spanish.

---

[1]The conditional tenses have been included because they have parallels in English. The subjunctive tenses have been omitted because they have no parallels in English.

Pattern (see *Tips for Learning Word Forms,* p. 5)

Start by comparing the forms of the new tense to the other forms of that verb you already know, particularly the forms that are close in spelling and/or pronunciation. For example, as you learn the preterite tense of regular -**ar** verbs like **comprar** *to buy*, compare the forms to the present tense which you have already learned.

1. Identify the similarities with the other tenses. This will help you remember the new tense.

PRESENT:		PRETERITE:	
compro		**compr**é	
compras		**compr**aste	
compra		**compr**ó	
compramos		**compr**amos	
compráis		**compr**asteis	
compran		**compr**aron	

- Stem is the same in the present and the preterite.
- 1ˢᵗ per. pl. is the same form in the present and preterite.

2. Identify the differences with the other tenses. This will help you avoid mixing them up.

- The preterite tense has accent marks on the 1ˢᵗ and 3ʳᵈ pers. sing. endings: compré, compró.
- An accent mark sometimes distinguishes the present tense from the preterite.

compro	1ˢᵗ pers. sing. present	*I buy*
compró	3ʳᵈ pers. sing. preterite	*he, she, you bought*

Flashcards

1. As you learn new tenses, separate the verb flashcards from your other cards and on the Spanish side note any irregular forms in that tense. If a verb has only one form that is irregular in a tense, make sure that you indicate that the other forms are regular.

> INFINITIVE: poner *to put*
> PRESENT: pongo (all other forms regular) *I put*
> PRETERITE STEM: pus-; no accent on 1ˢᵗ & 2ⁿᵈ per. sing. (puse, puso)
> STEM FUTURE/CONDITIONAL: pondr-

2. You will be able to recognize more patterns as you learn more verbs and tenses.

Practice

1. For simple tenses, see *Study Tips – Verb Conjugations,* p. 46.
2. For compound tenses, see *Study Tips – Perfect Tenses,* p. 85.
3. Apply the pattern you've just learned by writing and saying out loud another verb that follows the same pattern. For example, if you have learned that the irregular future stem of **poner** *(to put, place)* follows the "-**d** pattern," you can practice with other verbs with the same irregular future stem.

INFINITIVE	FUTURE STEM
poner	pondr-
tener (to have)	tendr-

4. Rewrite the practice sentences of a tense you've learned earlier using the new tense.

CHAPTER

WHAT IS THE PRESENT TENSE?

The **PRESENT TENSE** indicates that the action of the verb is happening at the present time, that is, at the moment the speaker is talking. The present tense can also indicate a habitual action or a general truth.

PRESENT MOMENT	I *see* you.
HABITUAL ACTION	He *smokes* constantly.
GENERAL TRUTH	The sun *rises* every day.

IN ENGLISH

There are three forms of the verb that indicate the present tense. Each form has a slightly different meaning.

PRESENT	Mary *studies* in the library.
PRESENT PROGRESSIVE	Mary *is studying* in the library.
PRESENT EMPHATIC	Mary *does study* in the library.

Depending on the information requested in a question, you will automatically choose one of the three forms above in your answer.

Where does Mary study? She *studies* in the library.
Where is Mary now? She *is studying* in the library.
Does Mary study in the library? Yes, she *does study* in the library.

IN SPANISH

The present tense in Spanish is a simple tense formed by adding a set of endings to the stem of the verb (see *What is a Verb Conjugation?*, p. 39). Your textbook will give you the present tense endings.

Unlike English, there is only one verb form to indicate the present tense. The Spanish present tense is used to express the meaning of the English present, present progressive, and present emphatic tenses.

*Mary **studies** in the library.*
estudia

*Mary **is studying** in the library.*
estudia

*Mary **does study** in the library.*
estudia

CAREFUL — Since the present is always indicated by the ending of the verb without an auxiliary verb such as *is* and *does*, you must not translate these English auxiliary verbs into Spanish. Simply put the main verb in the present tense.

CHAPTER

WHAT IS THE PAST TENSE?

¹ The **PAST TENSE** is used to express an action that occurred in the past.

> I *saw* you yesterday.

IN ENGLISH

There are several verb forms which indicate that the action took place in the past.

I worked	SIMPLE PAST
I was working	PAST PROGRESSIVE
I used to work	WITH HELPING VERB USED TO
I did work	PAST EMPHATIC
I have worked	PRESENT PERFECT
I had worked	PAST PERFECT

The simple past is a simple tense; that is, it consists of one word (*worked* in the example above). The other past tenses are compound tenses; that is, they consist of more than one word—an auxiliary plus a main verb *(was working, did work)*. The present and past perfect tenses are discussed in a separate section (see *What are Perfect Tenses?*, p. 82).

IN SPANISH

As in English, there are several verb tenses that indicate that an action took place in the past. Each tense has its own set of endings and its own rules as to when and how to use it. We are concerned here with only two of the past tenses in Spanish: the preterite (**el pretérito**) and the imperfect (**el imperfecto**).

THE PRETERITE

The preterite is a simple tense formed by adding a set of endings to the stem of the verb. There are many irregular verbs in the preterite tense. It is important to learn the preterite forms since the stem of the preterite is also used as the base for other verb forms.

The preterite generally translates as the simple past in English.

hablé	*I spoke*
estudié	*I studied*

THE IMPERFECT
The imperfect is a simple tense formed by adding a set of endings to the stem of the verb. The conjugation is very regular (there are only 3 irregular verbs in the imperfect): -**ar** verbs use one set of endings while -**er** and -**ir** verbs use another set of endings.

There are two English verb forms that indicate that the imperfect should be used in Spanish.

1. the English verb form includes, or could include, *used to*

> *When I was little, I played in the park.*
>
>   could be replaced by *used to play*
> Cuando yo era joven, **jugaba** en el parque.
>
>   imperfect

2. the English verb form is in the past progressive tense, as in *was playing, were studying*

> *I was studying in my room.*
> **Yo estudiaba** en mi cuarto.
>
>   imperfect

Except for these two verb forms, the tense of the English verb will usually not indicate whether you should use the imperfect or the preterite.

SELECTION OF THE PRETERITE OR THE IMPERFECT
When discussing and describing past events and activities, both the imperfect and the preterite are used. Whether to put a verb in the preterite or the imperfect often depends upon the context. As a general guideline, the difference in the two tenses is as follows:

> PRETERITE → tells "what happened" during a fixed period of time
>
> IMPERFECT → tells "how things used to be" or "what was going on" during a period of time

Here is an example. The same form of the verb *to go*, namely "went," is used in the two answers below. However, the tense of the Spanish verb **ir** *(to go)* changes depending on the question asked.

- "What happened?"

> QUESTION: *What **did** you **do** yesterday?*
> ANSWER: *I **went** to the park.*
>   The question and answer tell "what happened yesterday;"

40

50

60

70

therefore, the Spanish equivalent of *did do* and *went* are in the preterite.

QUESTION: ¿Qué **hiciste** ayer?
ANSWER: **Fui** al parque.

- "How things used to be"

    QUESTION: *What **did** you do when you were a child?*
    ANSWER: *I **went** to the park.*
    The question and answer tell "how things used to be;" therefore, the Spanish equivalent of *did do* and *went* are in the imperfect.

    QUESTION: ¿Qué **hacías** cuando eras joven?
    ANSWER: **Iba** al parque.

- "What was going on?"

    The imperfect and the preterite indicate actions that took place during the same time period in the past. You will often find the two tenses intermingled in a sentence or a story.

    *I **was reading** when he **arrived.***
    Both actions *reading* and *arrived* took place at the same time. What was going on? *I was reading* → imperfect. What happened? *He arrived* → preterite.
    Leía cuando **llegó.**
    imperfect   preterite

Consult your Spanish textbook for additional guidelines to help you choose the appropriate tense.

STUDY TIPS — THE PRETERITE

Patterns (see *Tips for Learning Word Forms,* p. 5 and *Study Tips – Verb Conjugations,* p. 46)

1. Regular verbs

    STEM: infinitive minus -**ar**, -**er**, or -**ir**
    ENDINGS: all have an accent on 1st and 3rd pers. sing.

    INFINITIVE: comprar *(to buy)*   volver *(to return)*   escribir *(to write)*
    STEM: compr-   volv-   escrib-

    | compré | compramos | volví | volvimos | escribí | escribimos |
    | compraste | comprasteis | volviste | volvisteis | escribiste | escribisteis |
    | compró | compraron | volvió | volvieron | escribió | escribieron |

    What similarities do you see? Here are some:
    - 1st pers. sing.: -**ar** verbs end in -**é**; -**er** and -**ir** verbs end in -**í**
    - 2nd pers. sing.: the endings of -**ar** and -**ir** verbs keep the vowel of the infinitive (-**a** and -**i**); the ending of -**er** verbs changes to -**i**
    - 3rd pers. sing.: all end in -**ó**; -**er** and -**ir** verbs add an -**i** before the -**ó**

- 1ˢᵗ pers. pl.: all end in **-mos**, the same as 1ˢᵗ pers. pl. of present tense
- 2ⁿᵈ pers. pl.: all end in **-steis**; the vowel preceding the **-steis** is the same as for 2ⁿᵈ pers. sing.
- 3ʳᵈ pers. pl.: all end in **-ron**; the ending of **-ar** verbs keeps the vowel of the infinitive (**-a-**); the endings of **-er** and **-ir** verbs change to **-ie-**

2. Irregular verbs

Many verbs are irregular in the preterite and have to be learned individually. Some of them, however, fall into a pattern based on irregularities in their stem, their endings, or both. Here are examples of verbs with irregular stems (the vowel of the stem changes to "u") and the irregular preterite endings added to all **u** stem preterites.

INFINITIVE: estar *(to be)*		saber *(to know)*		tener *(to have)*	
STEM: estuv-		sup-		tuv-	
estuve	estuvimos	supe	supimos	tuve	tuvimos
estuviste	estuvisteis	supiste	supisteis	tuviste	tuvisteis
estuvo	estuvieron	supo	supieron	tuvo	tuvieron

Look for similarities and differences between these endings for **u** stem verbs and the regular preterite endings above under 1.

Flashcards

On your verb cards add any irregular preterite stems and/or endings.

Practice

1. Sort out some verbs with regular preterite endings.
   - Look at the Spanish side. Write or say out loud sentences putting the verb in the preterite tense.
   - Look at the English side. Write or say out loud Spanish sentences putting the verb in the preterite tense.
2. Sort out all the verbs with irregular preterite stems and/or endings. Repeat the two steps under No. 1 above.
3. Mix the group of verbs that are regular and irregular in the preterite. Repeat the two steps under No. 1 above.

CHAPTER

WHAT ARE AUXILIARY VERBS?

1   A verb is called an AUXILIARY VERB or HELPING VERB when it helps
another verb, called the MAIN VERB, form one of its tenses.

He *has been gone* two weeks.	*has*	AUXILIARY VERB
	been	AUXILIARY VERB
	gone	MAIN VERB

IN ENGLISH

There are three auxiliary verbs, ***to have, to be***, and ***to do***,
as well as a series of auxiliary words such as ***will, would,
may, must, can, could*** that are used to change the tense
10   and meaning of the main verb.

- Auxiliaries are used primarily to indicate the tense of
the main verb (present, past, future — see *What is Meant
by Tense?*, p. 61).

| Mary *is* reading a book. | PRESENT |
| auxiliary *to be* | |

| Mary *has* read a book. | PAST |
| auxiliary *to have* | |

20
| Mary *will* read a book. | FUTURE |
| auxiliary *will* | |

- The auxiliary verb *to do* is used to help formulate questions and to make sentences negative (see *What are
Declarative and Interrogative Sentences?*, p. 54 and *What
are Affirmative and Negative Sentences?*, p. 51).

| *Does* Mary *read* a book? | INTERROGATIVE SENTENCE |
| Mary *does* not *read* a book. | NEGATIVE SENTENCE |

IN SPANISH
30   There are three verbs that can be used as auxiliary verbs:
estar *(to be)*, **haber** *(to have)*, and **ser** *(to be)*. The other English auxiliaries such as *do, does, did, will*, or *would* do not
exist as auxiliaries in Spanish. Their meaning is conveyed
either by a different structure or by the form of the main
verb. You will find more on this topic under the chapters
dealing with the different tenses.

A verb tense composed of an auxiliary verb plus a main verb is called a COMPOUND TENSE, as opposed to a SIMPLE TENSE which is a tense composed of only the main verb.

Julia **estudia**.

    simple tense
    present tense of **estudiar**

Julia studies.

Julia **ha estudiado**.

    auxiliary main
    verb   verb
    compound tense
    present perfect tense of **estudiar**

Julia has studied.

AUXILIARY VERBS USED TO INDICATE TENSE AND VOICE

The auxiliary verbs **estar, haber**, and **ser** conjugated in the different tenses are followed by the participle of the main verb (see *What is a Participle?*, 73) to form three types of compound tenses in Spanish.

Let us look at examples of some compound tenses.

PERFECT TENSES — The auxiliary verb **haber** *(to have)* followed by the past participle of the main verb is used to form the many perfect tenses (see p. 74 in *What is a Participle?* and *What are Perfect Tenses?*, p. 82).

- present perfect tense → present tense of **haber** + past participle of main verb

    Los estudiantes **han llegado**.

        auxiliary   main
        verb   verb
        haber   **llegar** *(to arrive)*

    The students have arrived.

- past perfect tense → imperfect tense of **haber** + past participle of main verb

    Los estudiantes ya **habían llegado**.

        auxiliary   main
        verb   verb
        haber   **llegar** *(to arrive)*

    The students had already arrived.

You will learn other perfect tenses as your study of Spanish progresses.

PROGRESSIVE TENSES — The auxiliary verb **estar** *(to be)* followed by the present participle of the main verb is used to form the progressive tenses (see *What is a Participle?*, p. 73 and *What are Progressive Tenses?*, p. 76).

- present progressive tense → present tense of **estar** + present participle of main verb

  Ahora mismo **estoy leyendo** un libro.

  auxiliary   main
  verb   verb
  estar   **leer** *(to read)*

  *Right now **I am reading** a book.*

- imperfect progressive tense → imperfect tense of **estar** + present participle of main verb

  Estábamos mirando una película.

  auxiliary   main
  verb   verb
  estar   **escuchar** *(to listen)*

  We were watching a movie.

You will learn other progressive tenses as your study of Spanish progresses.

PASSIVE VOICE — The auxiliary verb **ser** *(to be)* is used to form the passive voice (see *What is Meant by Active and Passive Voice?*, p. 103).

El puente **fue construido** por los romanos.

auxiliary   main verb
ser   **construir** *(to build)*

*The bridge **was built** by the Romans.*

WHAT IS A PARTICIPLE?

A **PARTICIPLE** is a form of a verb that can be used in one of two ways: with an auxiliary verb to indicate certain tenses or as an adjective to describe something.

> He *has closed* the door.
>
> auxiliary + participle → past tense
>
> He heard me through the *closed* door.
>
> participle describing *door* → adjective

There are two types of participles: the present participle and the past participle.

PRESENT PARTICIPLE
IN ENGLISH

The present participle is easy to recognize because it is the *-ing* form of the verb: *working, studying, dancing, playing.*

The present participle has two primary uses:

1. as the main verb following the auxiliary verb *to be* to indicate a progressive tense (see *What are Auxiliary Verbs?*, p. 70 and *What are Progressive Tenses?*, p. 76)

> She *is writing* a report with her new computer.
>
> present progressive of *to write*
>
> They *were sleeping.*
>
> past progressive of *to sleep*

2. as an adjective (see *What is an Adjective?*, p. 108)

> A pen is a *writing* instrument.
>
> describes the noun *instrument*
>
> He woke the *sleeping* child.
>
> describes the noun *child*

IN SPANISH

The present participle can be regular or irregular. Here are the endings of regular verbs:

- **-ar** verbs add **-ando** to the stem (see p. 44)
- **-er** and **-ir** verbs add **-iendo** to the stem

The **-ndo** of the Spanish participle corresponds to the *-ing* of the English present participle.

Here are examples of regular present participles:

INFINITIVE	STEM	PRESENT PARTICIPLE
cant**ar**	cant-	cant**ando**
com**er**	com-	com**iendo**
viv**ir**	viv-	viv**iendo**

There are some irregular forms that you will have to memorize individually.

The present participle is used primarily in the formation of the progressive tenses (see *What are Progressive Tenses?*, p. 76).

CAREFUL — Never assume that an English word ending in *-ing* will translate by its Spanish counterpart in **-ndo**.

PAST PARTICIPLE
IN ENGLISH
The past participle is formed in several ways. It is the form of the verb that follows *I have*: *I have **spoken**, I have **written**, I have **walked**.*

The past participle has two primary uses:

1. as the main verb following the auxiliary verb *to have* to indicate a past tense

   I *have written* all that I have to say.

   present perfect of *to write*

   He *had*n't *spoken* to me since our quarrel.

   past perfect of *to speak*

2. as an adjective

   Is the *written* word more important than the *spoken* word?

   describes the noun *word*   describes the noun *word*

IN SPANISH
The past participle can be regular or irregular. Here are the endings of regular verbs:

- **-ar** verbs add **-ado** to the stem
- **-er** and **-ir** verbs add **-ido** to the stem

The **-do** of the Spanish participle often corresponds to the *-ed* of the English past participle.

Here are examples of regular past participles:

INFINITIVE	STEM	PAST PARTICIPLE
cantar	cant-	cantado
comer	com-	comido
vivir	viv-	vivido

80

There are some irregular forms that you will have to memorize individually.

As in English, the past participle can be used as the main verb of a compound tense or as an adjective.

1. as the main verb in compound tenses with the auxiliary verb **haber** *(to have)* to indicate a perfect tense (see *What are Perfect Tenses?*, p. 82)

90

> Los estudiantes **han terminado** la lección.
> *The students **have finished** the lesson.*

2. as an adjective that agrees with the noun it modifies in gender and number

> *the **closed** door*
> > *Closed* modifies the noun *door*. Since **la puerta** *(door)* is feminine singular, the word for *closed* must be feminine singular. The participle must end with the letter **-a**.
> la puerta **cerrada**

100

> *the **stolen** cars*
> > *Stolen* modifies the noun *cars*. Since **los coches** *(cars)* is masculine plural, the word for *stolen* must be masculine plural. The participle must end with the letters **-os**.
> los coches **robados**

CHAPTER

WHAT ARE PROGRESSIVE TENSES?

1   **PROGRESSIVE TENSES** are used to talk about actions that are in progress at a specific moment in time; they emphasize the moment that an action takes place.

> John *is talking* on the phone.
>
> present progressive:
> emphasizes that the action is taking place right now

> We *were trying* to start the car.
>
> past progressive:
> emphasizes that the action was taking place at a specific time in
10   the past

IN ENGLISH

Progressive tenses are made up of the auxiliary verb *to be* + the present participle of the main verb (see *What is a Participle?*, p. 73).

> We *are leaving* right now.
>
> present participle of
> main verb *to leave*
> present tense of *to be*

20
> At that moment John *was washing* his car.
>
> present participle of
> main verb *to wash*
> past tense of *to be*

Notice that it is the tense of the auxiliary verb *to be* that indicates when the action of the main verb takes place.

> we *are* studying
>
> present tense of *to be* → present progressive

> we *were* studying
30
> past tense of *to be* → past progressive

IN SPANISH

The progressive tenses are made up of the auxiliary verb **estar** *(to be)* + the present participle of the main verb. All the tenses in Spanish have a progressive form. In this section we shall only look at the present progressive.

The present progressive is made up of the present tense of **estar** + the present participle of the main verb.

Estamos saliendo ahora mismo.

present tense present participle
of **estar** of **salir** *(to leave)*

We are leaving right now.

¿**Estás comiendo** ahora?

present tense present participle
of **estar** of **comer** *(to eat)*

Are you eating now?

USE OF THE PROGRESSIVE TENSES

The progressive tenses are used far more frequently in English than in Spanish.

In English, the progressive tenses are used for habitual actions, to state general truths, or to indicate that an action is happening at a specific moment (see *What is the Present Tense?*, p. 64).

In Spanish, the progressive tenses are only used for emphasis, for instance, to emphasize that an action is taking place at a particular moment, as opposed to another time, or to stress the continuity of an action. Where English uses the present progressive tense, Spanish often uses the present tense.

*John, what **are you studying** in school?*

English present progressive → Spanish present: **estudias**
You are asking what John is studying in general over a period of time.

*John, what **are you studying** now?*

English present progressive → Spanish present progressive: **estás estudiando**
The word *now* indicates that you want to know what John is studying at this particular time as opposed to all other times.

*Mary, **are you working** for the government?*

English present progressive → Spanish present: **trabajas**
You are asking where Mary is working in general over a period of time.

*Mary, **are you working** right now?*

English present progressive → Spanish present progressive: **estás trabajando**
The words *right now* indicate that you want to know if Mary is working at this particular time as opposed to all other times.

40

50

60

70

CHAPTER

WHAT IS THE FUTURE TENSE?

1   The **FUTURE TENSE** indicates that an action will take place some time in the future.

> Mary *will call* as soon as she gets home.
> <u>future</u>

IN ENGLISH

The future tense is formed with the auxiliary words *will* or *shall* + the dictionary form of the main verb. Note that *shall* is used in formal English (and British English) and *will* occurs in everyday language. In conversation *shall*
10   and *will* are often shortened to *'ll*.

> Paul and Mary *will do* their homework tomorrow.
> *I'll leave* tonight.

IN SPANISH

You do not need an auxiliary to show that an action will take place. The future tense is indicated by a simple tense.
Regular verbs use the infinitive as a stem for the future tense.

	INFINITIVE	STEM	
20	visitar	visitar-	*to visit*
	comer	comer-	*to eat*
	vivir	vivir-	*to live*

Irregular verbs have irregular future stems that you will have to memorize individually. Your textbook will list irregular future verb stems and give you the endings to be added in order to form the future tense.

SUBSTITUTE FOR THE FUTURE TENSE

30   In English and in Spanish an action that will occur some time in the future can also be expressed without using the future tense itself, but with a construction called the **IMMEDIATE FUTURE**.

IN ENGLISH

The immediate future is expressed with the verb *to go* in the present progressive tense + the infinitive of the main verb: *I am going to travel, she is going to dance.*

similar meaning

I am going to travel.   *I will travel.*

present progressive   future tense   40
of *to go* + infinitive

IN SPANISH

The same construction exists in Spanish; it is formed with the verb **ir** *(to go)* in the present tense + **a** + the infinitive of the main verb: **voy a viajar** *(I'm going to travel)*, **ella va a bailar** *(she's going to dance)*.

Look at the difference between the forms of the two constructions.

similar meaning

50

Voy a estudiar.   **Estudiaré.**

present of **ir** +   future tense
a + infinitive

I am going to study.   *I will study.*

present progressive   future tense
of *to go* + infinitive

CAREFUL — Note that the "**a**" has no English equivalent; it must appear in the Spanish sentence, however.

FUTURE OF PROBABILITY

60

In addition to expressing an action that will take place in the future, the future tense in Spanish can be used to express a probable fact, what the speaker feels is probably true. This is called the FUTURE OF PROBABILITY.

IN ENGLISH

The idea of probability is expressed with words such as *must, probably, wonder.*

> My keys *must* be around here.
> My keys are *probably* around here.
> I *wonder* if my keys are around here.

70

IN SPANISH

It is not necessary to use the words *must, probably,* or *wonder* to express probable facts; the main verb is simply put into the future tense.

> *I wonder what time it is.*
>
> present tense   main verb → present tense
>
> ¿Qué hora **será**?
>
> main verb future tense

It's probably 1:00 o'clock.
main verb *is* → present tense
Será la una.
main verb → future tense

*I can't find my book. John **must have** it.*
main verb → infinitive
No puedo encontrar mi libro. Juan lo **tendrá**.
main verb → future tense

STUDY TIPS — THE FUTURE TENSE

Patterns

1. Future stems (see *Tips for Learning Word Forms,* p. 5 and *Tips for Learning Vocabulary,* pp. 2-5).

   Regular stems: The infinitive form is the stem.
   Irregular stems: Stems must be learned as vocabulary.

2. Endings: All the verbs, regardless if they have a regular or an irregular stem, add the same endings.

INFINITIVE:	hablar	salir	
STEM:	hablar- *(reg.)*	saldr- *(irreg.)*	
	hablaré	saldré	saldremos
	hablarás	saldrás	saldéis
	hablará	saldrán	saldrán

INFINITIVE:	hablar		salir	
STEM:	hablar- *(reg.)*		saldr- *(irreg.)*	
	hablar**é**	hablar**emos**	saldr**é**	saldr**emos**
	hablar**ás**	hablar**éis**	saldr**ás**	saldr**éis**
	hablar**á**	hablar**án**	saldr**á**	saldr**án**

   What pattern do you see?
   - all forms have an accent, except the 1st pers. pl. form
   - in the ending, the vowel -e is used three times, in the 1st pers. sing. and the 1st and 2nd pers. pl.; the vowel -a is also used three times, in the 2nd and 3rd pers. sing. and the 3rd pers. pl.

Flashcards

On your verb card add the irregular future stem, if there is one. NOTE: The future stem will also be the stem for the conditional (see *What is the Conditional?,* p. 98).

decir	*to say, to tell*
dir-	(stem: future/conditional)
salir	*to leave*
saldr-	(stem: future/conditional)

Practice

1. Sort out some verbs with regular future stems.

   - Look at the Spanish side of the card. Write or say out loud sentences putting the verb in the future tense.
   - Look at the English side. Write or say out loud Spanish sentences putting the verb in the future tense.

2. Sort out the verbs with irregular future stems. Repeat the two steps under No. 1 above.

3. Mix the group of verbs with regular and irregular stems. Repeat the two steps under No. 1 above.

WHAT ARE PERFECT TENSES?

PERFECT TENSES are compound verbs made up of the auxiliary verb *to have* + the past participle of the main verb (see *What is a Participle?*, p. 73).

I *have* not *seen* him.
auxiliary   past participle
verb   of *to see*

They *had* already *gone.*
auxiliary   past participle
verb   of *to go*

IN ENGLISH

There are four perfect tenses formed with the auxiliary verb *to have* + the past participle of the main verb. The name of each perfect tense is based on the tense used for the auxiliary verb *to have.*

1. **Present perfect** — *to have* in the present tense + the past participle of the main verb (see *What is the Present Tense?*, p. 64).

I *have eaten.*
present   past participle
          of *to eat*

The boys *have washed* the car.
present past participle
         of *to wash*

2. **Past perfect (pluperfect)** — *to have* in the simple past + the past participle of the main verb (see *What is the Past Tense?*, p. 66).

I *had eaten* before six o'clock.
simple   past participle
past   of *to eat*

The boys *had washed* the car before the storm.
simple   past participle
past   of *to wash*

3. **Future perfect** — *to have* in the future tense + the past participle of the main verb (see *What is the Future Tense?*, p. 78).

> I *will have eaten* by six o'clock.
> └─┬─┘ │
> future   past participle
> of *to eat*

> The boys *will have washed* the car by Thursday.
> └─┬─┘ │
> future   past participle
> of *to wash*

4. **Conditional perfect** — *to have* in the conditional + the past participle of the main verb (see *What is the Conditional?*, p. 98).

> I *would have eaten* if I had had the time.
> └─┬─┘ │
> conditional   past participle
> of *to eat*

> John *would have washed* the car if he had been here.
> └─┬─┘ │
> conditional   past participle
> of *to wash*

IN SPANISH

The perfect tenses are made up of a form of the auxiliary verb **haber** *(to have)* + the past participle of the main verb. In Spanish there are several perfect tenses: four perfect tenses in the indicative mood (see *What is Meant by Mood?*, p. 86) and two in the subjunctive (see *What is the Subjunctive?*, p. 88). As in English, the name of the tense is based on the tense of the auxiliary verb **haber**.

We are listing the various perfect tenses here so that you can see the pattern that they follow. The perfect tenses are not always used the same way in Spanish as in English. Consult your Spanish textbook in order to learn to use them properly.

SPANISH PERFECT TENSES IN THE INDICATIVE MOOD

1. **Present perfect** (perfecto) — **haber** in the present tense + the past participle of the main verb. Generally the Spanish present perfect is used in the same way as the present perfect in English.

> **He comido.**
> *I have eaten.*

> Los chicos **han lavado** el coche.
> *The boys **have washed** the car.*

2. **Past perfect or Pluperfect** (pluscuamperfecto) — **haber** in the imperfect + the past participle of the main verb. The past perfect is used to express an action completed in the past before another past action or event. Generally, it is used the same way as in English.

> **Había comido** antes de las seis.
> *I **had eaten** before six o'clock.*

> Los chicos **habían lavado** el coche antes de la tempestad.
> *The boys **had washed** the car before the storm.*

3. **Future perfect** (futuro perfecto) — **haber** in the future + the past participle of the main verb. Generally, it is used the same way as in English.

> **Habré comido** para las seis.
> *I **will have eaten** by six o'clock.*

> Los chicos **habrán lavado** el coche para el jueves.
> *The boys **will have washed** the car by Thursday.*

4. **Conditional perfect** (condicional perfecto) — **haber** in the conditional + the past participle of the main verb.

> **Habría comido** si hubiera tenido tiempo.
> *I **would have eaten** if I had had time.*

> Los chicos **habrían lavado** el coche si hubieran estado aquí.
> *The boys **would have washed** the car if they had been here.*

SPANISH PERFECT TENSES IN THE SUBJUNCTIVE MOOD

1. **Present perfect subjunctive** (perfecto del subjuntivo) — **haber** in the present subjunctive + the past participle of the main verb. This tense is a present perfect used when a subjunctive is required.

> *He hopes that **they have arrived**.*
>
> requires that · present perfect subjunctive
> the following
> verb be in the subjunctive
> Espera que **hayan llegado**.

2. **Pluperfect subjunctive** (pluscuamperfecto del subjuntivo) — **haber** in the imperfect subjunctive + the past participle of the main verb. This tense is a past perfect used when a subjunctive is required.

> *He hoped that **they had arrived**.*
>
> requires that · pluperfect subjunctive
> the following
> verb be in the subjunctive
> Esperaba que **hubieran llegado**.

Patterns (see *Tips for Learning Word Forms,* p. 5 and *Tips for Learning Vocabulary,* pp. 2-5)

1. Review the conjugation of **haber** *(to have)* in the tenses you will need to form the various perfect tenses (see pp. 83-4).
   - present: he, has, ha, hemos, habéis, han
   - imperfect: había, habías, había, habíamos, habíais, habían
   - future: habré, habrás, habrá, habremos, habréis, habrán
   - conditional: habría, habrías, habría, habríamos, habríais, habrían
   - present subjunctive: haya, hayas, haya, hayamos, hayáis, hayan
   - imperfect subjunctive: hubiera, hubieras, hubiera, hubiéramos, hubierais, hubieran

2. Review the formation of past participles (see pp. 74-5).
   - regular past participle: **-ar** add **-ado** to the stem, **-er** and **-ir** add **-ido**
   - irregular past participle: To be learned as vocabulary.

Flashcards

Add the irregular past participle, if there is one, to the Spanish side of your verb flashcards.

Practice

PRESENT PERFECT TENSE

1. Sort out some verbs with regular past participles.
   - Look at the Spanish side. Write or say out loud sentences putting the verb into the present perfect tense.
   - Look at the English side. Write or say out loud Spanish sentences putting the verb into the present perfect tense.

2. Sort out the verbs with irregular past participles. Follow the steps under No. 1 above.

Follow the steps above to practice the past perfect (pluperfect), future perfect, and conditional perfect tenses.

CHAPTER

WHAT IS MEANT BY MOOD?

MOOD in the grammatical sense applies to verbs and indicates the attitude of the speaker toward what he or she is saying.

Different moods serve different purposes. For example, verbs that state a fact belong to one mood *(you are studying, you studied)*. The verb form that gives orders belongs to another mood *(Study!)*. Some moods have multiple tenses while others have only one tense.

You should recognize the names of the moods so that you will know what your Spanish textbook is referring to when it uses these terms. You will learn when to use the various moods as you learn verbs and their tenses.

IN ENGLISH

Verbs can be in one of three moods.

1. The **INDICATIVE MOOD** is used to state the action of the verb, that is, to *indicate* facts. This is the most common mood and most of the verb forms that you use in everyday conversation belong to the indicative mood. The majority of the tenses studied in this handbook belong to the indicative mood: for example, the present tense (see p. 64), the past tense (see p. 66), and the future tense (see p. 78).

> Robert *studies* Spanish.
> present indicative

> Anita *was* here.
> past indicative

> They *will arrive* tomorrow.
> future indicative

2. The **IMPERATIVE MOOD** is used to give commands or orders (see *What is the Imperative?*, p. 93). This mood is not divided into tenses.

> Robert, *study* Spanish now!
> Anita, *be* home on time!

3. The SUBJUNCTIVE MOOD is used to express an attitude or feeling toward the action of the verb; it is *subjective* about it (see *What is the Subjunctive?*, p. 88). In English this mood is not divided into tenses.

> The school requires that students *study* Spanish.
> I wish that Anita *were* here.
> The teacher recommends that he *do* his homework.

IN SPANISH

The Spanish language identifies two moods: the indicative and the subjunctive.

1. The INDICATIVE MOOD, as in English, is the most common and most of the tenses you will learn belong to this mood.

2. The SUBJUNCTIVE MOOD is used much more frequently in Spanish than in English. The Spanish subjunctive has four tenses: present, imperfect, present perfect, and past perfect (also called the pluperfect). In addition, most imperative or command forms are present subjunctive forms. Textbooks will use the term "present subjunctive" to distinguish that tense from the "present indicative."

When there is no reference to mood, the verb belongs to the most common mood, the indicative.

CHAPTER

WHAT IS THE SUBJUNCTIVE?

The **SUBJUNCTIVE** is a mood used to express a wish, hope, uncertainty, or other similar attitudes toward a fact or an idea. Since it stresses the subject's feelings about the fact or idea, it is usually *subjective* about them.

> I wish he *were* here.
> subject's   subjunctive
> wish

> The teacher insisted that the homework *be* neat.
> subject's   subjunctive
> attitude

IN ENGLISH

The subjunctive verb form is difficult to recognize because it is spelled like other tenses of the verb: the dictionary form or the simple past tense.

INDICATIVE	SUBJUNCTIVE
He *reads* a lot.	The course requires that he *read* a lot.
present indicative *to read*	subjunctive (same as dictionary form)
I *am* in Detroit right now.	I wish I *were* in Buenos Aires.
present indicative *to be*	subjunctive (same as simple past tense)

The subjunctive occurs most commonly in three kinds of sentences.

1. The subjunctive form of the verb *to be* (***were***), is used in the if-clause of hypothetical sentences (see pp. 99-101 in *What is the Conditional?* for an explanation of clauses).

> ⌐ if-clause ⌐   ⌐ result clause ⌐
> If I *were* in Europe now, I would go to Madrid.
> subjunctive

> ⌐ result clause ⌐   ⌐ if-clause ⌐
> John would run faster if he *were* in shape.
> subjunctive

2. The same subjunctive form *were* is used in statements expressing a wish.

> I wish I *were* in Europe right now.
> |
> subjunctive

> I wish she *were* my teacher.
> |
> subjunctive

3. The subjunctive form of all verbs is used following expressions that ask, demand, request, or express necessity.

> She asked that I *come* to see her.
> └──┬──┘ |
> request   subjunctive same as dictionary form

> It is necessary that you *study* a lot.
> └────┬────┘ |
> demand   subjunctive same as dictionary form

IN SPANISH

The subjunctive mood is used very frequently; unfortunately English usage will rarely help you decide where or how to use it in Spanish. It has many tenses in Spanish; however, in this section we shall only look at the present subjunctive.

Here are examples of verbs and expressions that require that the verb that follows be in the subjunctive, providing that the two verbs have different subjects (Ex. *"I am sorry you are late")*. If the first and second verbs have the same subject (Ex. *"I am sorry I am late")* the subjunctive is not required. Consult your textbook for additional examples.

Notice that the first verb or expression remains in the indicative; it is the second verb that is put in the subjunctive when it does not have the same subject as the first verb.

- a verb of wishing or wanting

> Quiero que Uds. **estudien** mucho.
> | |
> subject **yo**   subject **Uds.**
> **querer** *(to want)*   **estudiar** *(to study)*
> indicative   subjunctive
> *I want you **to study** a lot.*
> (word-for-word: *I want that **you study** a lot*)

- an expression of doubt or uncertainty

> Dudo que Roberto **llegue** hoy.
> | |
> subject **yo**   subject **Roberto**
> **dudar** *(to doubt)*   **llegar** *(to arrive)*
> indicative   subjunctive
> *I doubt that Robert **will arrive** today.*
> (word-for-word: *I doubt that Robert **arrives** today*)

40

50

60

70

- an impersonal expression

    Es posible que **compremos** un coche nuevo.

    subject "it"   subject **nosotros**
    es + adjective   **comprar** *(to buy)*
    indicative   subjunctive

    *It is possible that **we will buy** a new car.*
    (word-for-word: *It is possible that **we buy** a new car*)

- a verb of advice or command

    Te aconsejo que **comas** muchos vegetales.

    subject **yo**   subject **tú**
    aconsejar *(to advise)* **comer** *(to eat)*
    indicative   subjunctive

    *I advise **you to eat** a lot of vegetables.*
    (word-for-word: *I advise that **you eat** a lot of vegetables*)

- an expression of emotion

    Siento que Julio **esté** enfermo.

    subject **yo**   subject **él (Julio)**
    sentir *(to be sorry)* **estar** *(to be)*
    indicative   subjunctive

    *I am sorry that Julio **is** sick.*

CAREFUL — The tense and mood of an English verb rarely indicate if you should use the subjunctive in Spanish. As you can see in the examples above and below, a variety of English verb forms can require a subjunctive in a Spanish sentence.

- infinitive

    *I want you **to study** a lot.*
    Quiero que Uds. **estudien** mucho.

    *I advise you **to eat** a lot of vegetables.*
    Te aconsejo que **comas** muchos vegetales.

- future tense

    *I doubt that Roberto **will arrive** today.*
    Dudo que Roberto **llegue** hoy.

    *It is possible that **we will buy** a new car.*
    Es posible que **compremos** un coche nuevo.

- present tense

    *I'm sorry that Julio **is** sick.*
    Siento que Julio **esté** enfermo.

Patterns (see *Tips for Learning Word Forms* p. 5 and *Tips for Learning Vocabulary*, pp. 2-5)

1. Subjunctive stems
   - Regular stems: 1st pers. sing. (**yo** form) of the present indicative minus the –o ending

		Indicative present 1st pers. sing.	Subjunctive stem
hablar	*to speak*	hablo	habl-
comer	*to eat*	como	com-
escribir	*to write*	escribo	escrib-
tener	*to have*	tengo	teng-
salir	*to leave*	salgo	salg-

   - Irregular stems: To be learned as vocabulary.

2. Endings (see your textbook and *Study Tips – Verb Conjugations*, p. 46)
   - **-ar** verbs use the present indicative endings for **–er, -ir** verbs

hablar	hable	hablemos
	hables	habléis
	hable	hablen

   - **-er** and **–ir** verbs use the present indicative endings for **–ar** verbs

tener	tenga	tengamos	**salir**	salga	salgamos
	tengas	tengáis		salgas	salgáis
	tenga	tengan		salga	salgan

In summary, the present subjunctive is identifiable from the present indicative by the "traded" endings: verbs with "**a**" in the indicative endings have an "**e**" in the subjunctive endings and verbs with an "**e**" or "**i**" in the indicative endings have an "**a**" in the subjunctive endings.

Flashcards
On your verb cards, add the irregular subjunctive stem, if there is one.

ir	*to go*
vay- (subjunctive stem)	
saber	*to know*
sep- (subjunctive stem)	

On your verb cards, indicate the verbs that require that the verb of the second clause be in the subjunctive.

querer + subj.	*to want, to wish*
recomendar + subj.	*to recommend*

Practice
A. LEARNING THE SUBJUNCTIVE FORMS

1. Sort out verbs with regular subjunctive stems.
   - Look at the Spanish side. Write or say out loud sentences putting the verb in the present subjunctive.
   - Look at the English side. Write or say out loud Spanish sentences putting the verb in the present subjunctive.
2. Sort out verbs with irregular subjunctive stems. Repeat the two steps under No. 1 above.

3. Mix the group of verbs with regular and irregular subjunctive stems. Repeat the two steps under No. 1 above.

4. Using the group of verbs with regular and irregular subjunctive stems, write or say out loud the present indicative forms followed by the present subjunctive forms. This will help you to remember what distinguishes one from the other.

B. LEARNING TO USE THE SUBJUNCTIVE

1. Learn the verbs and expressions that require that the verb which follows be put in the subjunctive.

2. Sort out some verbs that require the use of the subjunctive in the second clause of the sentence.

   ■ Look at the Spanish side. Write or say out loud sentences with two clauses, the verb of the first clause requiring the subjunctive in the second clause.

   ■ Look at the English side. Write or say out loud Spanish sentences with two clauses, the verb of the first clause requiring the subjunctive in the second clause.

   > querer *to want, to wish*
   > Quiero que Juan **estudie** mucho.   *I want Juan **to study** a lot.*

   > dudar *to doubt*
   > Dudo que Juan **hable** inglés.   *I doubt that Juan **speaks** English.*

WHAT IS THE IMPERATIVE?

The IMPERATIVE is used to give an order. The AFFIRMATIVE IMPER-   1
ATIVE is an order to do something. The NEGATIVE IMPERATIVE is
an order not to do something.

> *Come* here!
> |
> affirmative command
>
> *Don't come* here!
> |___|
> negative command

IN ENGLISH

There are two types of commands, depending on who is   10
told to do, or not to do, something.

1. **"YOU" command** — When an order is given to one or
   more persons, the dictionary form of the verb is used.

AFFIRMATIVE IMPERATIVE	NEGATIVE IMPERATIVE
Answer the phone.	*Don't answer* the phone.
Clean your room.	*Don't clean* your room.
Speak softly.	*Don't speak* softly.

2. **"WE" command** — When an order is given to oneself as
   well as to others, the phrase "let's" (a contraction of *let
   us*) is used + the dictionary form of the verb.   20

AFFIRMATIVE IMPERATIVE	NEGATIVE IMPERATIVE
Let's leave.	*Let's not leave.*
Let's go to the movies.	*Let's not go* to the movies.

IN SPANISH

As in English, there are affirmative and negative commands.

1. **"YOU" command** — There are many forms of the "you"
   command to distinguish familiar and formal, as well as
   affirmative and negative.

   ▪ **"Tú" command** — When an order is given to a person   30
     to whom you say **tú**.
     The regular affirmative **tú** command has the same
   form as the 3rd person singular of the present indicative tense. There are also several irregular forms that
   you will have to learn individually. The negative **tú**
   command has the same form as the 2nd person singular of the present subjunctive.

AFFIRMATIVE IMPERATIVE	NEGATIVE IMPERATIVE
Habla.	No hables.
present indicative	present subjunctive
3rd pers. sing.	2nd pers. sing.
Speak.	*Don't speak.*

Ven aquí.	No vengas aquí.
irregular form	present subjunctive
	2nd pers. sing.
Come here.	*Don't come here.*

- "Vosostros" **command** — When an order is given to two or more persons to whom you say **tú** individually. The **vosotros** command is a familiar plural command and is used only in Spain.

    The affirmative **vosotros** command is formed by dropping the -**r** from the infinitive ending and replacing it with the letter -**d**. The negative **vosotros** command has the same form as the 2nd person plural of the present subjunctive.

AFFIRMATIVE IMPERATIVE	NEGATIVE IMPERATIVE
Venid aquí.	No vengáis aquí.
infinitive **venir** *(to come)*	present subjunctive
-**r** → -**d**	2nd per. pl.
Come here.	*Don't come here.*

Hablad.	No habléis.
infinitive **hablar** *(to speak)*	present subjunctive
-**r** → -**d**	2nd pers. pl·
Speak.	*Don't speak.*

- "Usted" **command** — When an order is given to a person to whom you say **usted**.

    Both the affirmative and negative **usted** commands have the same form as the 3rd person singular of the present subjunctive.

AFFIRMATIVE IMPERATIVE	NEGATIVE IMPERATIVE
Hable.	No hable.
present subjunctive	present subjunctive
3rd pers. sing.	3rd pers. sing.
Speak.	*Don't speak.*

Venga aquí.	No venga aquí.
present subjunctive	present subjunctive
3rd pers. sing.	3rd pers. sing.
Come here.	*Don't come here.*

80

■ **"Ustedes" command** — IN SPAIN: When an order is given to two or more persons to whom you say **usted** individually. IN LATIN AMERICA: When an order is given to two or more persons to whom you say **tú** or **usted** individually.

Both the affirmative and negative **ustedes** commands have the same form as the 3rd person plural of the present subjunctive.

90

AFFIRMATIVE IMPERATIVE	NEGATIVE IMPERATIVE
Hablen.	**No hablen.**
present subjunctive	present subjunctive
3rd pers. pl.	3rd pers. pl.
Speak.	*Don't speak.*

Vengan aquí.	No vengan aquí.
present subjunctive	present subjunctive
3rd pers. pl.	3rd pers. pl.
Come here.	*Don't come here.*

100

2. **"WE" command** — The affirmative and negative **nosotros** commands have the same form as the 1st person plural of the present subjunctive.

AFFIRMATIVE IMPERATIVE	NEGATIVE IMPERATIVE
Hablemos.	**No hablemos.**
present subjunctive	present subjunctive
1st pers. pl.	1st pers. pl.
Let's talk.	*Let's not talk.*

Salgamos.	No salgamos.
present subjunctive	present subjunctive
1st pers. pl.	1st pers. pl.
Let's leave.	*Let's not leave.*

110

Notice that the English phrase *let's* does not translate into Spanish; the command ending is the equivalent of *let's*.

In English and in Spanish the absence of the pronoun in the sentence is a good indication that you are dealing with an imperative and not a present tense (see *What is the Present Tense?*, p. 64).

120

You answer the phone.
|
present

Answer the phone.
|
imperative

SUMMARY

Here is a chart you can use as a reference for choosing the proper form of the Spanish command.

130

	COMMAND FORMS	
	AFFIRMATIVE	NEGATIVE
tú *you*	present **indicative** 3rd pers. sing.	present **subjunctive** 2nd pers. sing.
vosotros *you*	infinitive -**r** → -**d**	present **subjunctive** 2nd pers. pl.
usted *you*	present **subjunctive** 3rd pers. sing.	present **subjunctive** 3rd pers. sing.
ustedes *you*	present **subjunctive** 3rd pers. pl.	present **subjunctive** 3rd pers. pl.
nosotros *we*	present **subjunctive** 1st pers. pl.	present **subjunctive** 1st pers. pl.

STUDY TIPS — THE IMPERATIVE

Patterns

Look for a pattern in the chart of command forms above.

1. What is the form used: the present subjunctive, a modified infinitive, or the present indicative?
   - The present subjunctive is used for all forms, affirmative and negative, except the affirmative commands of **tú** and **vosotros**.
   - A modified infinitive with the final -**r** replaced by -**d** is used for the affirmative command of **vosotros**.
   - The present indicative is used for the affirmative command of **tú**.

2. What is the person used: the 2nd pers. sing., 3rd pers. sing., or the 1st pers. pl.?
   - as usual, **Ud.**, **Uds.** use the 3rd pers. sing. and pl.
   - as usual, **nosotros** uses the 1st pers. pl.
   - as usual, **tú** uses the 2nd pers. sing., but only for the negative
   - unusual, **tú** uses the 3rd pers. sing. for the affirmative
   - unusual, **vosotros** uses a modified infinitive which has no person

INFINITIVE: esperar *to hope*

	AFFIRMATIVE		NEGATIVE	
(tú)	espera	(IND. 3RD PERS. SING.)	no esperes	(SUBJ. 2ND PERS. SING.)
(vosotros)	esperad	(INF. -R → -D)	no esperéis	(SUBJ. 2ND PERS. PL.)
(Ud.)	espere	(SUBJ. 3RD PERS. SING.)	no espere	(SUBJ. 3RD PERS. SING.)
(Uds.)	esperen	(SUBJ. 3RD PERS. PL.)	no esperen	(SUBJ. 3RD PERS. PL.)
(nosotros)	esperemos	(SUBJ. 1ST PERS. PL.)	no esperemos	(SUBJ. 1ST PERS. PL.)

Flashcards

Since the imperative of a verb has such a variety of forms, it is advisable to write all the forms, negative and affirmative, on your flashcard so that you can review them. Negative forms can be in parentheses after the word "no."

INFINITIVE:	ir *to go*		empezar *to begin*	
(tú)	vé	(no vayas)	empieza	(no empieces)
(vosotros)	id	(no vayáis)	empezad	(no empecéis)
(Ud.)	vaya	(no vaya)	empiece	(no empiece)
(Uds.)	vayan	(no vayan)	empiecen	(no empiecen)
(nosotros)	vamos	(no vayamos)	empecemos	(no empecemos)

Practice

1. Sort out the verbs with regular imperative forms.

■ Look at the Spanish side. Write or say out loud the affirmative and negative command forms in a short sentence.

■ Look at the English side. Write or say out loud the affirmative and negative **tú** command forms of the equivalent Spanish verb in a sentence.

2. Repeat the above with irregular imperative forms.

CHAPTER

28

WHAT IS THE CONDITIONAL?

The conditional is a verb form using the auxiliary *would*.

> He *would like* to go.

THE CONDITIONAL
IN ENGLISH

The **CONDITIONAL** is a compound form made up of the auxiliary word ***would*** + the dictionary form of the main verb: *I would eat, he would come.*

The conditional is used in the following ways:

1. as a polite form with *like* and in polite requests

> I *would like* to eat.
>> More polite than "I want to eat."

> *Would* you close the door.
>> "Close the door" is softened by the use of *would*.

2. in an indirect statement to express a future-in-the-past

An **INDIRECT STATEMENT** repeats, or reports, but does not quote, someone's words, as opposed to a **DIRECT STATEMENT** which is a word-for-word quotation of what someone said. In written form a direct statement is always between quotation marks.

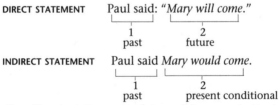

In the direct statement above, 2 is a quotation in the future tense. In the indirect statement, 2 is called a **FUTURE-IN-THE-PAST** because it is a future action relative to the past statement in the same sentence, i.e., Mary's coming is future to the time in the past when Paul spoke.

IN SPANISH

The conditional is a simple tense formed with the future stem (see p. 78) + the endings of the imperfect tense for **-er** and **-ir** verbs (see your textbook).

FUTURE STEM	CONDITIONAL	
hablar-	hablaría	*I would speak*
comer-	comería	*I would eat*
vivir-	viviría	*I would live*
pondr-	pondría	*I would put*
har-	haría	*I would do*

The conditional is used in the same ways as in English:

1. as a polite form or in polite requests

Querría un vaso de agua.
conditional
***I would like** a glass of water.*

¿**Podría** Ud. cerrar la puerta, por favor?
conditional
***Would** you close the door, please?*

2. in an indirect statement to express a future-in-the-past

Pablo dijo que **vendría.**
conditional
*Paul said (that) **he would come.***

CONDITIONAL PERFECT

IN ENGLISH

The **CONDITIONAL PERFECT** is a compound tense formed with the auxiliaries ***would have*** + past participle of the main verb: *I would have eaten, he would have come* (see "contrary-to-fact statements," pp. 100-1).

IN SPANISH

The conditional perfect is a compound tense formed with the conditional of **haber** *to have* + the past participle of the main verb: **habría comido** *I would have eaten,* **habría venido** *he would have come.*

"IF-CLAUSES"

The term "if-clauses" refers to complex sentences consisting of two clauses (see p. 48-9 and p. 50 in *What are Sentences, Clauses, and Phrases?*):

1. a condition clause — A subordinate clause which is introduced by *if.*
2. a result clause — A main clause which is the result of the condition above.

The result clause can precede or follow the condition clause.

If he wins this race, it will be a surprise.
It will be a surprise if he wins this race.

There are two types of "if-clauses": 1. on-going conditions and 2. contrary-to-fact statements.

ON-GOING CONDITIONS — The condition could be true anytime, in the present, past or future. The condition clause can come before or after the result clause.

IN ENGLISH

The initial "if" in on-going conditions means "any time," and could be replaced by *when, whenever.* Depending on the tense of the condition, the verb of the result clause will be in the present, future or past.

> *If/When/Whenever* I have money, I spend it.
> present   present

> *If/When/Whenever* I have money, I will spend it.
> present   future

> *If/When/Whenever* I had money, I spent it.
> past   past

> On-going condition: Anytime I have money
> Result: I spend it.

IN SPANISH

While English can have different words at the beginning of on-going conditions, in Spanish on-going conditions always start with **cuando** *(when).* Depending on the tense of the on-going condition, the verb of the result clause will be in the present or the past.

> *If/when/whenever I have money, I spend it.*
> **Cuando** tengo dinero, lo gasto.
> present   present

> *If I have money, I will spend it.*
> **Cuando** tengo dinero, lo gasto.
> present   present (with future meaning)

> *If I had money, I spent it.*
> **Cuando** tenía dinero, lo gastaba.
> imperfect   imperfect

CONTRARY-TO-FACT STATEMENTS — There is no possibility of the condition being realized since it refers to the past. The condition clause can come before or after the result clause.

IN ENGLISH

Contrary-to-fact statements are easily identifiable by the use of the conditional form of the verb in the result clause. The conditional is tied to the result clause, regardless if it is at the beginning or the end of the sentence.

- condition clause — always starts with *if*

  If he had known the truth, he *would have spoken.*
    Condition: He did not know the truth and there is no way the past can be changed → contrary-to-fact statement.

- result clause — the verb is in the conditional or the perfect conditional (see examples below).

  He *would have spoken*, if he had known the truth.

IN SPANISH

As in English, the result clause, regardless if it is at the beginning or the end of the sentence, has a verb in the conditional.

- condition clause — always starts with **si** *if.* In addition, the verb of the condition clause is in the subjunctive mood: the imperfect subjunctive or the pluperfect subjunctive.

- result clause — the verb is in the conditional or the conditional perfect.

In both in English and Spanish, the tenses of the verbs in the result and condition clauses depend on one another (see the charts below).

	RESULT CLAUSE	CONDITION CLAUSE
ENGLISH ⎫	conditional	simple past
SPANISH ⎭		imperfect subjunctive

I would go to the party if I had time.
 ⎿_____⏌ ⎿____⏌
 conditional   simple past

Iría a la fiesta si **tuviera** tiempo,
 ⏐   ⏐
 conditional   imperfect subjunctive

	RESULT CLAUSE	CONDITION CLAUSE
ENGLISH ⎫	conditional perfect	past perfect
SPANISH ⎭		pluperfect subjunctive

They would have received better grades if they had studied.
 ⎿_____⏌ ⎿_____⏌
 conditional perfect   past perfect

Habrían recibido mejores notas si **hubieran estudiado.**
 ⎿_____⏌ ⎿_____⏌
 conditional perfect   pluperfect subjunctive

130

140

150

160

CAREFUL — Be sure to distinguish between:

- *if* (*when, whenever*) **cuando** and *if* **si**:

    If I have the money, I go to the movies.
    Cuando tengo el dinero, voy al cine.

    If I have the money, I will go to the movies.
    Si tengo el dinero, iré al cine.

- *would* as part of the conditional form of a verb and *would* meaning *used to*, a past tense (see p. 67).

    He said he *would go* to Europe.

    future-in-the-past → conditional → **iría**

    If I had money, I *would go* to Europe.

    contrary-to-fact → conditional → **iría**

    When I was a child, I *would go* to Europe.

    past tense → imperfect → **iba**

WHAT IS MEANT BY ACTIVE
AND PASSIVE VOICE?

VOICE in the grammatical sense refers to the relationship
between the verb and its subject. There are two voices,
the ACTIVE VOICE and the PASSIVE VOICE.

ACTIVE VOICE — A sentence is said to be in the active voice
when the subject is the performer of the action of the verb.
In this instance, the verb is called an ACTIVE VERB.

> The teacher prepares the exam.
>   S   V   DO

> Paul ate an apple.
>   S V   DO

> Lightning has struck the tree.
>   S   V   DO

In these examples the subject (S) performs the action of the
verb (V) and the direct object (DO) is the receiver of the
action (see *What is a Subject?,* p. 28 and *What are Objects?,*
p. 138).

PASSIVE VOICE — A sentence is said to be in the passive voice
when the subject is the receiver of the action of the verb. In
this instance, the verb is called a PASSIVE VERB.

> The exam is prepared by the teacher.
>   S   V   agent

> The apple was eaten by Paul.
>   S   V   agent

> The tree has been struck by lightning.
>   S   V   agent

In these examples, the subject is the receiver of the action of
the verb. The performer of the action, if it is mentioned, is
introduced by the word "by" and is called the AGENT.

IN ENGLISH

The passive voice is expressed by the verb *to be* conjugated
in the appropriate tense + the past participle of the main

verb (see *What is a Participle?*, 73). The tense of the passive sentence is indicated by the tense of the verb *to be*.

> The exam *is prepared* by the teacher.
> present

> The exam *was prepared* by the teacher.
> past

> The exam *will be prepared* by the teacher.
> future

IN SPANISH

As in English, a passive verb can be expressed by the auxiliary verb **ser** *(to be)* conjugated in the appropriate tense + the past participle of the main verb. The tense of the passive sentence is indicated by the tense of the verb **ser**.

> El examen **es** preparado por el profesor.
> present
> *The exam is prepared by the teacher.*

> El examen **fue** preparado por el profesor.
> past
> *The exam was prepared by the teacher.*

> El examen **será** preparado por el profesor.
> future
> *The exam will be prepared by the teacher.*

In the passive voice formed with **ser** all past participles agree in gender and number with the subject.

> Esas **cartas** fueron **escritas** por el profesor.
> fem. pl.   fem. pl.
> *Those letters were written by the teacher.*

MAKING AN ACTIVE SENTENCE PASSIVE

The steps to change an active sentence to a passive sentence are the same in English and in Spanish.

1. The direct object of the active sentence is made the subject of the passive sentence.

> ACTIVE   The teacher prepares *the exam.*
>   direct object
> PASSIVE   *The exam* is prepared by the teacher.
>   subject

2. The tense of the verb of the active sentence is reflected
   in the tense of the verb *to be* in the passive sentence.

ACTIVE   The teacher *prepares* the exam.
                             |
                          present

PASSIVE   The exam *is* prepared by the teacher.
                       |
                    present

ACTIVE   The teacher *prepared* the exam.
                             |
                           past
PASSIVE   The exam *was* prepared by the teacher.
                       |
                     past

ACTIVE   The teacher *will* prepare the exam.
                           |
                         future
PASSIVE   The exam *will be* prepared by the teacher.
                     |___|
                     future

3. The subject of the active sentence is made the agent of
   the passive sentence introduced with *by*.

ACTIVE   *The teacher* prepares the exam.
                          |
                       subject
PASSIVE   The exam is prepared *by the teacher*.
                                    |
                                  agent

AVOIDING THE PASSIVE VOICE IN SPANISH

Although Spanish has a passive voice, whenever possible
Spanish speakers try to avoid it by replacing it with an
active construction. This is particularly true for general
statements when we don't know who is doing the action.

> English *is spoken* in many countries.
> We don't know who is speaking.

> The New York Times *is sold* here.
> We don't know who is selling.

There are two ways a passive sentence can be avoided in
Spanish.

1. using the "**se** construction" — The word **se** corresponds
   to the English indefinite pronoun *one* used in a general
   sense as in the sentence "*One* should eat when *one* is
   hungry." Spanish often makes *one* the subject of an
   active sentence, even in cases where English speakers
   would never use such a construction.

*English **is spoken** in many countries.*

"one speaks"
Se habla inglés en muchos países.

*The New York Times **is sold** here.*

"one sells"
Se vende el New York Times aquí.

130   2. using the 3rd person plural of the verb — The main verb of the sentence is changed from the English passive voice to the equivalent Spanish verb in the 3rd person plural. (The "they" corresponds to a general subject, such as *"They* say Mexico is very interesting.") The subject of the English sentence becomes the direct object in the Spanish sentence.

*English **is spoken** in many countries.*

subject + passive verb →
*"**they speak** English"*

140

3rd pers. pl. + active verb + DO
Hablan inglés en muchos países.

*The New York Times **is sold** here.*

subject + passive verb →
*"**they sell** the New York Times"*

3rd pers. pl. + active verb + DO
Venden el New York Times aquí.

150   **CAREFUL** — Make sure you distinguish between the auxiliary **haber** *(to have)* + the past participle used to form a past tense in the active voice (see *What are Perfect Tenses?*, p. 82) and **ser** *(to be)* + the past participle used to form a passive sentence. For example, **ha cerrado** is a past tense of the verb **cerrar** *(to close)* in the active voice and **fue cerrado** is a past tense in the passive voice. As you can see in the following examples, the same changes occur in English.

ACTIVE   *The teacher **has** prepared the exam.*

auxiliary *to have* → past (present perfect)

160

PASSIVE   *The exam **was** prepared by the teacher.*

auxiliary *to be* → past

ACTIVE

PASSIVE

El profesor **ha** escrito el examen.

auxiliary **haber** *(to have)* → past (present perfect)

El examen **fue** escrito por el profesor.

auxiliary **ser** *(to be)* → past

WHAT IS AN ADJECTIVE?

An **ADJECTIVE** is a word that describes a noun or a pronoun. There are different types of adjectives which are classified according to the way they describe a noun or pronoun.

DESCRIPTIVE ADJECTIVE — A descriptive adjective indicates a quality; it tells what kind of noun it is (see p. 109).
> She read an *interesting* book.
> He has *brown* eyes.

POSSESSIVE ADJECTIVE— A possessive adjective shows possession; it tells whose noun it is (see p. 117).
> *His* book is lost.
> *Our* parents are away.

INTERROGATIVE ADJECTIVE — An interrogative adjective asks a question about a noun (see p. 125).
> *What* book is lost?
> *Which* book did you read?

DEMONSTRATIVE ADJECTIVE — A demonstrative adjective points out a noun (see p. 127).
> *This* teacher is excellent.
> *That* question is very appropriate.

IN ENGLISH
English adjectives usually do not change their form, regardless of the noun or pronouns described.

IN SPANISH
The principal difference between English and Spanish adjectives is that while English adjectives do not change their form, Spanish adjectives change in order to agree in gender and number with the noun or pronoun they modify.

STUDY TIPS – DESCRIPTIVE ADJECTIVES (SEE P. 111)

STUDY TIPS – POSSESSIVE ADJECTIVES (SEE P. 123)

WHAT IS A DESCRIPTIVE ADJECTIVE?

A **DESCRIPTIVE ADJECTIVE** is a word that indicates a quality of a   1
noun or pronoun. As the name implies, it *describes* the noun
or pronoun.

> The book is *interesting.*
> | |
> noun   descriptive
> described adjective

IN ENGLISH

A descriptive adjective does not change form, regardless of
the noun or pronoun it modifies.

> The students are *intelligent.*   10
> She is an *intelligent* person.
>
> > The form of the adjective *intelligent* remains the same
> > although the persons described are different in number *(stu-dents* is plural and *person* is singular).

Descriptive adjectives are divided into two groups
depending on how they are connected to the noun they
modify.

1. A **PREDICATE ADJECTIVE** is connected to the noun it
   describes, always the subject of the sentence, by **LINKING**   20
   VERBS such as *to be, to feel, to look.*

   > The children are *good.*
   > | | |
   > noun   linking predicate
   > described verb   adjective

   > The house looks *small.*
   > | | |
   > noun   linking predicate
   > described verb   adjective

2. An **ATTRIBUTIVE ADJECTIVE** is connected directly to the
   noun it describes and always precedes it.   30

   > The *good* children were praised.
   > | |
   > attributive noun
   > adjective   described

   > The family lives in a *small* house.
   > | |
   > attributive noun
   > adjective   described

IN SPANISH

As in English, descriptive adjectives can be identified as predicate or attribute adjectives according to the way they are connected to the noun they describe.

Spanish descriptive adjectives differ in two important ways from English descriptive adjectives.

1. While English descriptive adjectives never change form, all Spanish descriptive adjectives, predicate and attributive, change form in order to agree in gender and number with the noun or pronoun they modify.

   Most adjectives change the final "**-o**" of the masculine singular form to "**-a**" to make the feminine form and add "**-s**" to the masculine singular or the feminine singular form to make it plural.

*the **red** car*	el coche **rojo**
	masc. masc.
	sing. sing.
*the **red** table*	la mesa **roja**
	fem. fem. (final -o → -a)
	sing. sing.
*the **red** cars*	los coches **rojos**
	masc. masc. (**rojo** + **-s**)
	pl. pl.
*the **red** tables*	las mesas **rojas**
	fem. fem. (**roja** + **-s**)
	pl. pl.

2. While English descriptive adjectives always come before the noun they modify, most, but not all, Spanish descriptive adjectives come after the noun they modify.

   Ella lee un libro **interesante**.
   *She is reading an **interesting** book.*

   However, some common Spanish descriptive adjectives come before the noun they modify.

   Juan es un **buen** chico.
   *John is a **good** boy.*

Your textbook will tell you, and you will have to learn, which Spanish descriptive adjectives precede and which follow the noun they modify.

NOUNS USED AS ADJECTIVES

Occasionally, a noun is used as an adjective; that is, it is used
to modify another noun.

IN ENGLISH

When a noun is used to describe another noun, the structure is as follows: the describing noun (adjective) + the noun described.

Spanish is easy.   The *Spanish* class is crowded.
| | |
noun   adjective noun described

Chemistry is difficult.   The *chemistry* books are expensive.
| | |
noun   adjective noun described

IN SPANISH

It is important that you recognize a noun acting as an
adjective because it remains a noun and does not change
form. In the examples below, you will see that the noun
described and the noun acting as an adjective have different genders and numbers.

When a noun is used as an adjective, the structure is as
follows: the noun described + **de** *(of)* + the describing
noun (adjective) without an article.

the Spanish class   →   la **clase** de **español**
| | | |
el español   la clase   fem. sing.   masc. sing.
                                  noun   noun/adjective
                                  described

the chemistry books →   los **libros** de **química**
| | | |
la química   los libros   masc. pl.   fem. sing.
                                  noun   noun/adjective
                                  described

STUDY TIPS — DESCRIPTIVE ADJECTIVES

Flashcards (see *Tips for learning Vocabulary*, pp. 2-5)

1. Create flashcards indicating the adjective twice on the Spanish side,
   once modifying a masculine noun and once modifying a feminine
   noun. This will show you the masculine and feminine forms of the
   adjective.

   un coche **rojo**   *a red car*
   una mesa **roja**   *a red table*

2. If the adjective has irregular singular or plural forms, illustrate them.

   el hombre **español**   *the Spanish man*
   los hombres **españoles**   *the Spanish men*

   la mujer **española**   *the Spanish woman*
   las mujeres **españolas**   *the Spanish women*

Practice

Write short sentences in Spanish using the descriptive adjectives you have learned, concentrating on the agreement of the adjectives with the nouns they modify.

WHAT IS MEANT BY COMPARISON OF ADJECTIVES?

The term COMPARISON OF ADJECTIVES is used when two or more   1
persons or things have the same quality (height, size, color,
any other characteristic) and we want to show which of
these persons or things has a greater, lesser, or equal degree
of that quality.

> comparison of adjectives
>
> Paul is *tall* but Mary is *taller.*
>
> adjective   adjective
> modifies *Paul*   modifies *Mary*
>
> Both nouns, Paul and Mary, have the same quality indi-   10
> cated by the adjective *tall,* and we want to show that Mary
> has a greater degree of that quality (i.e., she is *taller* than
> Paul).

In English and in Spanish there are two types of comparison:
comparative and superlative.

COMPARATIVE

The comparative compares a quality of one person or thing
with the same quality in another person or thing. The comparison can indicate that one or the other has more, less, or   20
the same amount of that quality.

IN ENGLISH

Let's go over the three degrees of comparison:

1. The comparison of GREATER DEGREE (more) is formed differently depending on the length of the adjective being
   compared.

   ▪ short adjective + *-er* + *than*

     Paul is tall*er than* Mary.
     Susan is old*er than* her sister.   30

   ▪ *more* + longer adjective + *than*

     Mary is *more* intelligent *than* John.
     His car is *more* expensive *than* ours.

2. The comparison of LESSER DEGREE (less) is formed as follows: *not as* + adjective + *as*, or *less* + adjective + *than*.

Mary is *not as* tall *as* Paul.
My car is *less* expensive *than* your car.

3. The comparison of EQUAL DEGREE (same) is formed as follows: *as* + adjective + *as*.

Robert is *as* tall *as* Mary.
My car is *as* expensive *as* his car.

IN SPANISH

As in English, the comparative has the same three degrees of comparison of adjectives.

Like all Spanish adjectives, Spanish comparative adjectives agree with the noun they modify. Although comparative adjectives refer to more than one noun or pronoun, they agree with the first noun or pronoun mentioned.

1. The comparison of GREATER DEGREE is formed as follows: **más** *(more)* + adjective + **que** *(than)*.

María es **más alta que** Juan.
        agrees with first noun mentioned → María
*Mary is **taller than** John.*

2. The comparison of LESSER DEGREE is formed as follows: **menos** *(less)* + adjective + **que** *(than)*.

Juan es **menos alto que** María.
        agrees with first noun mentioned → Juan
*John is **less tall than** Mary.*

3. The comparison of EQUAL DEGREE is formed as follows: **tan** *(as)* + adjective + **como** *(as)*.

María es **tan alta como** Roberto.
        agrees with first noun mentioned → María
*Mary is **as tall as** Robert.*

Note that in Spanish the first *as* is expressed with **tan** while the second *as* is expressed with **como**.

SUPERLATIVE

The superlative is used to stress the highest or lowest degrees of a quality.

IN ENGLISH

Let's go over the two degrees of the superlative:

1. The superlative of GREATEST DEGREE is formed differently depending on the length of the adjective.

- *the* + short adjective + *-est*

  Mary is *the* smart*est*.
  My car is *the* cheap*est* on the market.

- *the most* + long adjective

  Mary is *the most* intelligent.
  His car is *the most* expensive.

2. The superlative of LOWEST DEGREE is formed as follows: *the least* + adjective.

   Paul is *the least* active.
   Her car is *the least* expensive of all.

IN SPANISH

There are the same two degrees of the superlative:

1. The superlative of GREATEST DEGREE is formed as follows: **el, la, los** or **las** (depending on the gender and number of the noun described) + **más** *(most)* + adjective.

   Juan es **el más bajo** de la familia.
   masc. sing.
   *John is **the shortest** in the family.*

   María es **la más alta**.
   fem. sing.
   *Mary is **the tallest**.*

   Carlos y Roberto son **los más divertidos** de la clase.
   masc. pl.
   *Charles and Robert are **the funniest** in the class.*

   Teresa y Gloria son **las más simpáticas**.
   fem. pl.
   *Teresa and Gloria are **the nicest**.*

2. The superlative of LOWEST DEGREE is formed as follows: **el, la, los** or **las** (depending on the gender and number of the noun described) + **menos** *(least)* + adjective.

   Mi coche es **el menos caro**.
   masc. sing.
   *My car is **the least expensive**.*

120

CAREFUL — In English and in Spanish, a few adjectives have irregular forms of comparison which you will have to memorize individually.

ADJECTIVE	Esta manzana es **buena.**
	*This apple is **good.***
COMPARATIVE	Esta manzana es **mejor.**
	*This apple is **better.***
SUPERLATIVE	Esta manzana es **la mejor.**
	*This apple is **the best.***

WHAT IS A POSSESSIVE ADJECTIVE?

A **POSSESSIVE ADJECTIVE** is a word that describes a noun by
showing who possesses that noun.

> Whose house is that? It's *my* house.
>> *My* shows who possesses the noun *house*. The
>> possessor is "me." The object possessed is *house*.

IN ENGLISH

Like subject pronouns, possessive adjectives are identified
according to the person they represent (see p. 32).

> **SINGULAR POSSESSOR**
> | | | |
> |---|---|---|
> | 1ˢᵗ PERSON | | my |
> | 2ᴺᴰ PERSON | | your |
> | 3ᴿᴰ PERSON | MASCULINE | his |
> | | FEMININE | her |
> | | NEUTER | its |
>
> **PLURAL POSSESSOR**
> | | |
> |---|---|
> | 1ˢᵗ PERSON | our |
> | 2ᴺᴰ PERSON | your |
> | 3ᴿᴰ PERSON | their |

A possessive adjective changes to identify the possessor,
regardless of the objects possessed.

> Is that John's house? Yes, it is *his* house.
> Is that Mary's house? Yes, it is *her* house.
>> Although the object possessed is the same *(house)*, different
>> possessive adjectives *(his* and *her)* are used because the pos-
>> sessors are different *(John* and *Mary)*.

> Is that John's house? Yes, it is *his* house.
> Are those John's keys? Yes, they are *his* keys.
>> Although the objects possessed are different *(house* and
>> *keys)*, the same possessive adjective *(his)* is used because the
>> possessor is the same *(John)*.

IN SPANISH

Like English, a Spanish possessive adjective changes to
identify the possessor, but unlike English it also agrees,
like all Spanish adjectives, in gender and number with the
noun possessed.

For example, in the phrase **nuestro hermano** *(our brother)* the possessor *(our)* is indicated by the first letters of the 1ˢᵗ person plural possessive adjective **nuestr-**, and the gender and number of the noun possessed, **hermano** *(brother)*, which is masculine singular, is reflected in the masculine singular ending **-o**. Let us see what happens when we change *our brother* to *our sister*.

> *We love **our sister**.*
> Queremos a **nuestra hermana**.

$$\text{1}^{st}\text{ pers. pl.} \quad \text{fem. sing. ending}$$
> 1ˢᵗ pers. pl.
> possessor

> The first letters **nuestr-** remain the same because the possessor is still the 1ˢᵗ person plural, but the ending changes to **-a** to agree with **hermana** *(sister)* which is feminine singular.

Spanish has two sets of possessive adjectives: the STRESSED POSSESSIVE ADJECTIVES and the UNSTRESSED POSSESSIVE ADJECTIVES. The short, unstressed forms are the most common and will be considered first.

SPANISH UNSTRESSED POSSESSIVE ADJECTIVES

My, your *(tú, usted, ustedes* forms), **his, her, their**
In Spanish, each of the above possessive adjectives has two forms, a singular and a plural form. You will choose the one that agrees with the number of the noun possessed.

To choose the correct form of the possessive adjective:

1. Indicate the possessor. This is shown by the first two letters of the possessive adjective.

my	**mi**
your [tú form]	**tu**
his	
her	
your [usted form]	**su**
their	
your [ustedes form]	

2. Choose the ending according to the number of the noun possessed.

   - noun possessed is singular → the form of the possessive adjective does not change

   Ana lee **mi** libro. *Ana reads **my** book.*

   noun possessed singular

   Ana lee **tu** libro. *Ana reads **your** book.*
   Ana lee **su** libro. *Ana reads **her** (**his, your, their**) book.*

- noun possessed is plural → add -s to the possessive adjective

Ana lee **mis** libros.　　*Ana reads **my** books.*
   noun possessed plural

Ana lee **tus** libros.　　*Ana reads **your** books.*
Ana lee **sus** libros.　　*Ana reads **her** (**his, your, their**) books.*

Because the possessive adjective **su** has many meanings, Spanish speakers often replace it with the phrase: noun + **de** + pronoun.

	el libro **de él**	***his*** book
	el libro **de ella**	***her*** book
	el libro **de Ud.**	***your*** book
su libro	el libro **de ellos**	***their*** book
	el libro **de ellas**	***their*** book
	el libro **de Uds.**	***your*** book

You will have to rely on context to establish the English equivalent of the possessive adjectives **su** and **sus**.

Let us apply the above steps to examples:

*I am looking for **my** car.*

   1. POSSESSOR: *my* → 1st pers. sing. → **mi**
   2. NUMBER NOUN POSSESSED: **coche** *(car)* → singular
   3. SELECTION: **mi**

Busco **mi** coche.

*I am looking for **my** keys.*
   1. POSSESSOR: *my* → 1st pers. sing. → **mi**
   2. NUMBER NOUN POSSESSED: **llaves** *(keys)* → plural
   3. SELECTION: **mi-** + **-s**

Busco **mis** llaves.

Our, your (*vosotros* form)

In Spanish, the two possessive adjectives above have four forms, a masculine singular, a feminine singular, a masculine plural, and a feminine plural. You will choose the one that agrees with the gender and number of the noun possessed.

To choose the correct form of the possessive adjective:

1. Indicate the possessor. This is shown by the first letters of the possessive adjective.

   our　　　　　　　　**nuestr-**
   your [**vosotros** form]　　**vuestr-**

2. Choose the ending according to the gender and number of the noun possessed.

- noun possessed is masculine singular → add -o

  Ana lee **nuestro** libro. *Ana reads **our** book.*

      noun possessed masc. sing.

  Ana lee **vuestro** libro. *Ana reads **your** book.*

- noun possessed is feminine singular → add -a

  Ana lee **nuestra** revista. *Ana reads **our** magazine.*

      noun possessed fem. sing.

  Ana lee **vuestra** revista. *Ana reads **your** magazine.*

- noun possessed is masculine plural → add -os

  Ana lee **nuestros** libros. *Ana reads **our** books.*

      noun possessed masc. pl.

  Ana lee **vuestros** libros. *Ana reads **your** books.*

- noun possessed is feminine plural → add -as

  Ana lee **nuestras** revistas. *Ana reads **our** magazines.*

      noun possessed fem. pl.

  Ana lee **vuestras** revistas. *Ana reads **your** magazines.*

Let us apply the above steps to examples:

*We are looking for **our** car.*
1. POSSESSOR: *our* → 1ˢᵗ pers. pl. → **nuestr-**
2. GENDER & NUMBER NOUN POSSESSED: **coche** *(car)* → masc. sing.
3. SELECTION: **nuestr- + -o**

Buscamos **nuestro** coche.

*We are looking for **our** keys.*
1. POSSESSOR: *our* → 1ˢᵗ pers. pl. → **nuestr-**
2. GENDER & NUMBER NOUN POSSESSED: **llaves** *(keys)* → fem. pl.
3. SELECTION: **nuestr- + -as**

Buscamos **nuestras** llaves.

Notice that unstressed possessive adjectives are placed before the noun they modify.

CAREFUL — Make sure that the ending of possessive adjectives agrees with the noun modified and not with the possessor.

SPANISH STRESSED POSSESSIVE ADJECTIVES

Spanish also has another set of possessive adjectives called **STRESSED POSSESSIVE ADJECTIVES**. They are used to add emphasis to the possessor and correspond to the English "of mine," "of yours," etc.

Where is that *dress of mine?*

instead of *my dress*

Where are those *books of yours?*

instead of *your books*

The use of these stressed forms is more common in Spanish than in English.

The stressed possessive adjectives have four forms, a masculine singular, a feminine singular, a masculine plural, and a feminine plural. You will choose the one that agrees with the gender and number of the noun possessed.

To choose the correct stressed possessive adjective:

1. Indicate the possessor. This is shown by the first letters of the possessive adjective.

mine, of mine	**mí-**
your, of yours [**tú** form]	**tuy-**
his, of his her, of hers your, of yours [**usted** form]	**suy-**
our, of ours	**nuestr-**
your, of yours [**vosotros** form]	**vuestr-**
their, of theirs your, of yours [**ustedes** form]	**suy-**

2. Choose the ending according to the gender and number of the noun possessed.
   - noun possessed is masculine singular → add **-o**

     Ana lee un libro **mío.**

     noun possessed masc. sing.
     Ana is reading a book of mine.

   - noun possessed is feminine singular→ add **-a**

     Ana lee una revista **mía.**

     noun possessed fem. sing.
     Ana is reading a magazine of mine.

   - noun possessed is masculine plural → add **-os**

     Ana lee unos libros **míos.**

     noun possessed masc. pl.
     Ana is reading some books of mine.

170

180

190

200

- noun possessed is feminine plural → add -**as**

Ana lee unas revistas **mías**.
|
noun possessed fem. pl.

*Ana is reading some magazines **of mine**.*

Let us apply the above steps to examples:

My car is in the garage.
1. POSSESSOR: *my* → 1st pers. sing. → **mí-**
2. GENDER & NUMBER NOUN POSSESSED: **coche** (*car*) → masc. sing.
3. SELECTION: **mí- + -o**

El coche **mío** está en el garaje.

*These chairs **of yours** are very comfortable.*
1. POSSESSOR: *of yours* → 2nd pers. sing. → **tuy-**
2. GENDER & NUMBER NOUN POSSESSED: **sillas** (*chairs*) → fem. pl.
3. SELECTION: **tuy- + -as**

Estas sillas **tuyas** son muy cómodas.

Notice that stressed possessive adjectives are placed after the noun they modify.

SUMMARY

Here are two charts you can use as a reference.

POSSESSOR		UNSTRESSED POSSESSIVE ADJECTIVES	
		NOUN POSSESSED	
		SINGULAR	PLURAL
my	MASC. FEM.	mi	mis
your [tú form]	MASC. FEM.	tu	tus
his, her, your [usted form]	MASC. FEM.	su	sus
our	MASC. FEM.	nuestro nuestra	nuestros nuestras
your [vosotros form]	MASC. FEM.	vuestro vuestra	vuestros vuestras
their, your [ustedes form]	MASC. FEM.	su	sus

POSSESSOR	STRESSED POSSESSIVE ADJECTIVES		
	NOUN POSSESSED		
		SINGULAR	PLURAL
my, of mine	MASC.	mío	míos
	FEM.	mía	mías
your [tú form]	MASC.	tuyo	tuyos
	FEM.	tuya	tuyas
his, her, *your* [usted form]	MASC.	suyo	suyos
	FEM.	suya	suyas
our	MASC.	nuestro	nuestros
	FEM.	nuestra	nuestras
your [vosotros form]	MASC.	vuestro	vuestros
	FEM.	vuestra	vuestras
their, *your* [ustedes form]	MASC.	suyo	suyos
	FEM.	suya	suyas

250

STUDY TIPS — POSSESSIVE ADJECTIVES

Pattern (see *Tips for Learning Word Forms,* p. 5)

Flashcards

1. Create one card for each of the persons (1ˢᵗ, 2ⁿᵈ, and 3ʳᵈ sing. and pl.) with an example of the different forms of the unstressed possessive adjectives.

mi coche, **mis** coches	*my car, my cars*
mi casa, **mis** casas	*my house, my houses*
tu coche, **tus** coches	*your car, your cars*
tu casa, **tus** casas	*your house, your houses*
nuestro coche, **nuestros** coches	*our car, our cars*
nuestra casa, **nuestras** casas	*our house, our houses*

2. On the card for the 3ʳᵈ person, to reinforce the fact that *his, her, your,* and *their* can be either **su** or **sus** and that possessive adjectives agree with the thing possessed and not with the possessor, write short Spanish sentences with 3ʳᵈ person possessive adjectives modifying masculine and feminine nouns in the singular and plural.

Juan vende **su libro**.	*John sells **his (her, your, their) book**.*
Ana vende **su libro**.	*Ana sells **his (her, your, their) book**.*
Juan vende **su casa**.	*John sells **his (her, your, their) house**.*
Ana vende **su casa**.	*Ana sells **his (her, your, their) house**.*
Juan vende **sus libros**.	*John sells **his (her, your, their) books**.*
Ana vende **sus libros**.	*Ana sells **his (her, your, their) books**.*
Juan vende **sus casas**.	*John sells **his (her, your, their) houses**.*
Ana vende **sus casas**.	*Ana sells **his (her, your, their) houses**.*

3. Repeat steps No. 1 and 2 above with the stressed possessive adjectives.

Practice

1. Sort out your noun flashcards and select a few masculine and feminine nouns.

- Look at the Spanish side and go through the cards writing down or saying out loud the noun preceded by the correct forms of the unstressed possessive adjectives.

  el cuarto   *room*
  mi cuarto, tu cuarto, su cuarto, nuestro cuarto, vuestro cuarto
  la casa   *house*
  mi casa, tu casa, su casa, nuestra casa, vuestra casa
  los libros   *books*
  mis libros, tus libros, sus libros, nuestros libros, vuestros libros

- Look at the Spanish side and go through the cards writing down or saying out loud the noun with the correct forms of the stressed possessive adjectives.

  el cuarto   *room*
  el cuarto mío, el cuarto tuyo, el cuarto suyo, el cuarto nuestro, el cuarto vuestro

2. Use these noun cards to practice the forms for the 3rd pers. sing. and pl. (*his, her, your, their*) going from English to Spanish.

  his room, *her* room, *your* room, *their* room   **su** cuarto

WHAT IS AN INTERROGATIVE ADJECTIVE?

An **INTERROGATIVE ADJECTIVE** is a word that asks for information about a noun.

> *Which* book do you want?
>
> asks information about the noun *book*

IN ENGLISH

The words **which** and **what** are called interrogative adjectives when they come in front of a noun and are used to ask a question about that noun.

> *Which* instructor is teaching the course?
> *What* courses are you taking?

IN SPANISH

There are two interrogative adjectives: 1. **qué** which corresponds to the English *which* or *what* and 2. the forms of **cuánto** meaning *how much* or *how many*.[1]

1. *which* or *what* + noun → **qué** + noun

Qué is invariable; that is, it does not change form.

> ¿**Qué** revista lees?
> *What magazine are you reading?*
>
> ¿**Qué** libros quieres?
> *Which books do you want?*

2. *how much* or *how many* + noun → **cuánto** + noun

Cuánto changes forms to agree in number and gender with the noun it modifies. Therefore, in order to choose the correct form of **cuánto**, begin by analyzing the noun modified.

- noun modified is masculine singular → **cuánto**

> ¿**Cuánto** dinero necesitas?
> **Dinero** *(money)* is masculine singular, so the word for "how much" must be masculine singular.
> *How much money do you need?*

---

[1] **Qué** is used in standard Spanish. In certain areas of the Spanish-speaking world **cuál** and **cuáles** can function as interrogative adjectives: ¿**Cuál** libro quieres? *Which book do you want?*

- noun modified is feminine singular → **cuánta**

    ¿Cuánta sopa quieres?
    > **Sopa** *(soup)* is feminine singular, so the word for "how much" must be feminine singular.

    *How **much** soup do you want?*

- noun modified is masculine plural → **cuántos**

    ¿Cuántos discos tienes?
    > **Discos** *(CDs)* is masculine plural, so the word for "how many" must be masculine plural.

    *How **many** CDs do you have?*

- noun modified is feminine plural → **cuántas**

    ¿Cuántas maletas traes?
    > **Maletas** *(suitcases)* is feminine plural, so the word for "how many" must be feminine plural.

    *How **many** suitcases are you bringing?*

CAREFUL — The word *what* is not always an interrogative adjective. It can also be an interrogative pronoun (see *What is an Interrogative Pronoun?*, p. 169). When it is a pronoun, *what* (**qué**) is not followed by a noun.

> ***What** is on the table?*
> interrogative pronoun
> **¿Qué** hay en la mesa?

The expression "how many" is not always an interrogative adjective. It can also be an interrogative pronoun. When it is a pronoun, *how many* (**cuánto**) is not followed by a noun.

> *How **many** do you need?*
> interrogative pronoun
> **¿Cuántos** necesitas?

It is important that you distinguish interrogative adjectives from interrogative pronouns because, in Spanish, sometimes different words are used and they follow different rules.

WHAT IS A DEMONSTRATIVE ADJECTIVE?

A **DEMONSTRATIVE ADJECTIVE** is a word used to point out a noun.   1

> *This* book is interesting.
>
> points out the noun *book*

IN ENGLISH

The demonstrative adjectives are ***this*** and ***that*** in the singular and ***these*** and ***those*** in the plural. They are rare examples of English adjectives that agree in number with the noun they modify: *this* changes to *these* and *that* changes to *those* when they modify a plural noun.   10

Singular	Plural
this cat	*these* cats
that man	*those* men

This and *these* refer to persons or objects near the speaker, and *that* and *those* refer to persons or objects away from the speaker.

IN SPANISH

There are three sets of demonstrative adjectives and they all agree in gender and number with the nouns they modify.

In order to say *"this* house" or *"that* room" start by determining where the person or object is in relation to the   20
speaker or the person spoken to. Then, determine the gender and number of the noun you wish to point out and make the demonstrative adjective agree with that noun.

1. noun near the speaker (*this, these*) → a form of **este**
   - noun modified is masculine singular → **este**

     Este cuarto es grande.

     > **Cuarto** *(room)* is masculine singular, so the word for "this" must be masculine singular.

     This room is large.   30

   - noun modified is feminine singular → **esta**

     Esta casa es grande.

     > **Casa** *(house)* is feminine singular, so the word for "this" must be feminine singular.

     This house is large.

- noun modified is masculine plural → **estos**

  Estos cuartos son grandes.

  > **Cuartos** *(rooms)* is masculine plural, so the word for "these" must be masculine plural.

  These rooms are large.

- noun modified is feminine plural → **estas**

  Estas casas son grandes.

  > **Casas** *(houses)* is feminine plural, so the word for "these" must be feminine plural.

  These houses are large.

2. noun near the person spoken to (*that, those*) → a form of **ese**

- noun modified is masculine singular → **ese**

  Ese cuarto es grande.

  > **Cuarto** *(room)* is masculine singular, so the word for "that" must be masculine singular.

  That room is large.

- noun modified is feminine singular → **esa**

  Esa casa es grande.

  > **Casa** *(house)* is feminine singular, so the word for "that" must be feminine singular.

  That house is large.

- noun modified is masculine plural → **esos**

  Esos cuartos son grandes.

  > **Cuartos** *(rooms)* is masculine plural, so the word for "those" must be masculine plural.

  Those rooms are large.

- noun modified is feminine plural → **esas**

  Esas casas son grandes.

  > **Casas** *(houses)* is feminine plural, so the word for "those" must be feminine plural.

  Those houses are large.

3. noun away from both the speaker and the person spoken to (*that, those*) → a form of **aquel**

  Since English does not have this third set of demonstrative adjectives, there is no good translation for them. Sometimes "over there" is added to imply the distance.

- noun modified is masculine singular → **aquel**

  Aquel cuarto es grande.

  > **Cuarto** *(room)* is masculine singular, so the word for "that" must be masculine singular.

  *That room (**over there**) is large.*

- noun modified is feminine singular → **aquella**

  Aquella casa es grande.   80
  > **Casa** *(house)* is feminine singular, so the word for "that" must be feminine singular.

  *That house **(over there)** is large.*

- noun modified is masculine plural → **aquellos**

  Aquellos cuartos son grandes.
  > **Cuartos** *(rooms)* is masculine plural, so the word for "those" must be masculine plural.

  *Those rooms **(over there)** are large.*

- noun modified is feminine plural → **aquellas**

  Aquellas casas son grandes.   90
  > **Casas** *(houses)* is feminine plural, so the word for "those" must be feminine plural.

  *Those houses **(over there)** are large.*

CAREFUL — These three sets of demonstrative adjectives may also function as demonstrative pronouns (see *What is a Demonstrative Pronoun?*, p. 177). As demonstrative pronouns they are not followed by a noun.

CHAPTER

WHAT IS AN ADVERB?

An **ADVERB** is a word that describes a verb, an adjective, or another adverb. It indicates manner, degree, time, place.[1]

Mary drives *well.*

verb   adverb

The house is *very* big.

adverb adjective

The girl ran *too quickly.*

adverb   adverb

IN ENGLISH

There are different types of adverbs:

- an **ADVERB OF MANNER** answers the question *how?* Adverbs of manner are the most common and they are easy to recognize because they end with *-ly*.

  Mary sings *beautifully.*

  > *Beautifully* describes the verb *sings*; it tells you how Mary sings.

- an **ADVERB OF DEGREE** answers the question *how much?*

  Paul did *well* on the exam.

- an **ADVERB OF TIME** answers the question *when?*

  He will come *soon.*

- an **ADVERB OF PLACE** answers the question *where?*

  The children were left *behind.*

IN SPANISH

Most adverbs of manner can be recognized by the ending **-mente** which corresponds to the English ending *-ly*.

fácil**mente**	*easily*
natural**mente**	*naturally*
rápida**mente**	*rapidly*

---

[1]In English and in Spanish, the structure for comparing adverbs is the same as the structure for comparing adjectives (see *What is Meant by Comparison of Adjectives?*, p. 113).

You will have to memorize adverbs as vocabulary items. The most important fact for you to remember is that adverbs are INVARIABLE; ie., they never change form.

CAREFUL — Remember that in English *good* is an adjective since it modifies a noun and *well* is an adverb since it modifies a verb.

> The student writes *good* English.
>> *Good* modifies the noun *English;* it is an adjective.

> The student writes *well.*
>> *Well* modifies the verb *writes;* it is an adverb.

Likewise, in Spanish **bueno** is an adjective meaning *good;* **bien** is the adverb meaning *well.*

> *The **good** students speak Spanish **well.***
>   adjective   adverb
>
> Los estudiantes **buenos** hablan **bien** el español.
>   masc. pl. adj.   adverb

40

STUDY TIPS — ADVERBS

Flashcards (see *Tips for Learning Vocabulary,* pp. 2-5)

1. Create flashcards for each Spanish adverb that you learn; indicate its English equivalent.

siempre	*always*
rápidamente	*rapidly, quickly*

2. Add sample sentences illustrating the adverb within a sentence.

Manuel viene a clase **siempre**.	*Manuel **always** comes to class.*
Ana maneja **rápidamente**.	*Ana drives **fast (rapidly)**.*

WHAT IS A CONJUNCTION?

A **CONJUNCTION** is a word that links two or more words or groups of words.

> He had to choose between good *and* evil.
>
conjunction

> They left *because* they were bored.
>
conjunction

IN ENGLISH

There are two kinds of conjunctions: coordinating and subordinating.

- a **COORDINATING CONJUNCTION** joins words, phrases (groups of words without a verb), and clauses (groups of words with a verb) that are equal; it *coordinates* elements of equal rank. The major coordinating conjunctions are *and, but, or, nor, for,* and *yet.*

  > good *or* evil
  >
word   word

  > over the river *and* through the woods
  >
phrase   phrase

  > They invited us *but* we couldn't go.
  >
clause   clause

  In the last example, each of the two clauses, "they invited us" and "we couldn't go," expresses a complete thought; therefore, each clause could stand alone. When a clause expresses a complete thought and can stand alone, it is called a **MAIN CLAUSE**. In the above sentence, the coordinating conjunction *but* links two main clauses.

- a **SUBORDINATING CONJUNCTION** joins a main clause to a dependent clause; it *subordinates* one clause to another. A **DEPENDENT CLAUSE** does not express a complete thought; therefore, it cannot stand alone. There are various types of dependent clauses. A clause introduced by a subordinating conjunction is called a **SUBOR-**

DINATE CLAUSE. Typical subordinating conjunctions are *before, after, since, although, because, if, unless, so that, while, that,* and *when.*

subordinate clause   main clause

Although we were invited, we didn't go.

subordinating
conjunction

main clause   subordinate clause

They left *because* they were bored.

subordinating
conjunction

main clause   subordinate clause

He said *that* he was tired.

subordinating
conjunction

In the above examples, "although we were invited," "because they were bored," and "that he was tired," are all subordinate clauses. They are not complete thoughts and each is introduced by a subordinating conjunction.

Notice that the subordinate clause may come either at the beginning of the sentence or after the main clause (see *What are Sentences, Clauses, and Phrases?*, p. 48).

IN SPANISH

As in English, there are two types of conjunctions: coordinating and subordinating. In general conjunctions function in Spanish as they do in English. Conjunctions must be memorized as vocabulary items. Just as adverbs and prepositions, conjunctions are INVARIABLE; i.e., they never change their form.

STUDY TIPS — CONJUNCTIONS AND THE SUBJUNCTIVE

Flashcards (see *Tips for Learning Vocabulary*, pp. 2-5)

1. Create flashcards indicating Spanish conjunctions and their English equivalent.

pero	*but*
porque	*because*
y	*and*

2. When you learn the subjunctive (see *What is the Subjunctive*, p. 88), on the conjunction cards indicate the ones that are followed by the subjunctive instead of the indicative. Add an example as a reinforcement.

para que (+ subj.)   *in order to, so that*
Mi madre trabaja **para que**   *My mother works **so that***
  yo pueda ir a la universidad.   *I can go to the university.*

Practice

Write a series of sentences using various conjunctions. Make sure to put the verb that follows the conjunction in the subjunctive, if the conjunction requires it.

WHAT IS A PREPOSITION?

A **PREPOSITION** is a word that shows the relationship of one   1
word (usually a noun or pronoun) to another word (usually
another noun or pronoun) in the sentence.

prepositional phrase

Paul has an appointment *after* school.

preposition   object of preposition

The noun or pronoun following the preposition is called the
OBJECT OF THE PREPOSITION (see *What are Object of Preposition Pro-*
nouns?, p. 154). The preposition plus its object is called a
PREPOSITIONAL PHRASE.   10

IN ENGLISH
Prepositions normally indicate location, direction, or time.

- prepositions showing location or direction

> Paul was *in* the car.
> Mary put the books *on* the table.
> The students came directly *from* class.
> Mary went *to* school.

- prepositions showing time and date   20

> Many Spanish people go on vacation *in* August.
> *On* Mondays, they go to the university.
> I'm meeting him *at* 4:30 today.
> We're studying *before* the exam.
> Most people work *from* nine *to* five.

Other frequently used prepositions are: *during, since, with,*
between, of, about. Some prepositions are made up of more
than a single word: *because of, in front of, instead of, due to,*
in spite of, on account of.

IN SPANISH   30
Prepositions are identifed the same way as they are in
English. As in English, they are used to show the relation-
ship of one word to another in a sentence.

- Prepositions are **INVARIABLE**, that is, they never change
  form.

- You will have to memorize prepositions as vocabulary, paying special attention to their meaning and use. For example, the English preposition *for* has two equivalents in Spanish: **por** and **para**. Consult your Spanish textbook to learn how to distinguish between the two and when to use them.

CAREFUL — Prepositions can be tricky. Every language uses prepositions differently. Do not assume that the same preposition is used in Spanish as in English, or even that a preposition will be needed in Spanish when you must use one in English and vice versa.

ENGLISH	SPANISH
PREPOSITION	DIFFERENT PREPOSITION
to laugh *at*	reirse **de** *(of)*
to consist *of*	consistir **en** *(in)*
PREPOSITION	NO PREPOSITION
to look *for*	buscar
to look *at*	mirar
NO PREPOSITION	PREPOSITION
to leave	salir **de**
to enter	entrar **en**

A dictionary will usually give you the verb and the preposition which follows it, when one is required.

Do not translate an English verb + preposition with a word-for-word Spanish equivalent (see pp. 26-7).

STUDY TIPS — PREPOSITIONS

Flashcards (see *Tips for Learning Vocabulary,* pp. 2-5)
Be careful when creating flashcards for prepositions because one English preposition can have several Spanish equivalents and vice versa. Always learn a preposition in a short sentence illustrating its usage.

1. Prepositions indicating the position of one object or person in relation to another are the easiest to learn because there is usually only one Spanish equivalent.

sobre	*on top of*
El libro está **sobre** la mesa.	*The book is **on top of** the table.*
detrás de	*behind*
Juan está **detrás de** María.	*John is **behind** Mary.*

2. Prepositions such as **a, de, en** have many English equivalents because their meaning varies according to the noun that follows. Indicate their varied meanings on the English side of the card.

a (+ location)	to + location
Voy **a** la universidad.	I'm going **to** the university.
a (+ time)	at + time
Salgo **a** las diez.	I'm leaving **at** ten o'clock.
en (+ location)	on + location, at + location
El libro está **en** el escritorio.	The book is **on** the desk.
Juan está **en** el restaurante.	John is **at** the restaurant.

3. When you learn a verb that is usually followed by a particular preposition, indicate the preposition on the verb card and write a short sentence to illustrate its use.

entrar en	to enter
Entramos en la oficina	**We entered** the office
a las ocho.	at eight o'clock.

Practice

1. Following the examples under No. 1 above, think of two objects (or persons) and write Spanish sentences using prepositions placing the objects (or persons) in various positions in relation to one another.

Juan está **enfrente de** Carlos.	Juan is **in front of** Carlos.
Juan está **al lado de** Carlos.	Juan is **next to** Carlos.

2. Following the examples under No. 2 above, create short sentences using **a** + location, **en** + location, and **a** + time.

No voy **a** la fiesta.	I'm not going **to** the party.
Ricardo está **en** la biblioteca.	Ricardo is **at** the library.
La clase empieza **a** las nueve.	The class begins **at** nine (o'clock).

CHAPTER

WHAT ARE OBJECTS?

OBJECTS are nouns or pronouns indicating towards what or whom the action of the verb is directed.

Paul writes a *letter.*
verb   object

He speaks to *Mary.*
verb   object

The boy left with *his father.*
verb   object

There are three types of objects: direct objects, indirect objects, and objects of a preposition. In this chapter we have limited the examples to noun objects. For examples with pronoun objects see *What are Direct Object Pronouns?*, p. 144, *What are Indirect Object Pronouns?*, p. 148, and *What are Object of Preposition Pronouns?*, p. 154.

DIRECT OBJECT
IN ENGLISH

A direct object is a noun or pronoun that receives the action of the verb directly, without a preposition between the verb and the noun or pronoun. It answers the question *whom?* or *what?* asked after the verb.[1]

John sees *Mary.*
John sees *whom?* Mary.
Mary is the direct object.

John writes *a letter.*
John writes *what?* A letter.
A letter is the direct object.

Verbs can be classified as to whether or not they take a direct object.

- a **TRANSITIVE VERB** is a verb that takes a direct object. It is indicated by the abbreviation *v.t. (verbo transitivo)* in Spanish dictionaries.

---

[1]In this section, we will consider active sentences only (see *What is Meant by Active and Passive Voice?*, p. 103).

The boy *threw* the ball.

     transitive   direct object

- an **INTRANSITIVE VERB** is a verb that does not require a direct object. It is indicated by the abbreviation *v.i. (verbo intransitivo)* in Spanish dictionaries.

    Paul *is sleeping*.

        intransitive

IN SPANISH

As in English, a direct object is a noun or pronoun that receives the action of the verb directly. It answers the question **¿quién?** *(whom?)* or **¿qué?** *(what?)* asked after the verb.

    Juan escribe **una carta.**
        John writes *what?* A letter (**una carta**).
        Una carta is the direct object.
    *John writes **a letter**.*

In Spanish a direct object noun referring to a person is preceded by the word "**a.**" This is called the **PERSONAL a**. It does not have an English translation.

    Juan ve **a María.**

        personal **a** + direct object noun (person)
    *John sees **Mary**.*

    Juan ve **a las muchachas.**

        personal **a** + direct object noun (persons)
    *John sees **the girls**.*

    Juan ve **al hombre.**

        personal **a** + **el** + direct object noun (person)
    *John sees **the man**.*

    Juan ve **la casa.**

        no personal **a** required, direct object noun (thing)
    *John sees **the house**.*

INDIRECT OBJECT
IN ENGLISH

An indirect object is a noun or pronoun that receives the action of the verb indirectly. It answers the question *to whom?* or *to what?* asked after the verb.

John wrote *his brother.*
He wrote *to whom?* His brother.
His brother is the indirect object.

Sometimes the word *to* is included in the English sentence.[1]
John spoke *to Paul and Mary.*
John speaks *to whom?* To Paul and Mary.
Paul and Mary are two indirect objects.

IN SPANISH

As in English, an indirect object is a noun or pronoun that receives the action of the verb indirectly with the preposition **a** *(to)* relating it to the verb. It answers the question **¿a quién?** *(to whom)* or **¿a qué?** *(to what?)* asked after the verb.

In Spanish, when an indirect object noun refers to a person an indirect object pronoun must be added before the verb. For instance, **le** is used when the indirect object noun is singular and **les** is used when the indirect object noun is plural (see *What are Indirect Object Pronouns?*, p. 148).

Juan **le** escribió a su hermano.
|
singular
(word-for-word: *John (**to him**) wrote **to his brother***)
*John wrote (**to**) his brother.*

Juan **les** habló a Pablo y a María.
|
plural
(word-for-word: *John (**to them**) spoke **to Paul and Mary***)
*John spoke (**to**) Paul and Mary.*

SENTENCES WITH A DIRECT AND AN INDIRECT OBJECT

A sentence may contain both a direct object and an indirect object which may be either nouns or pronouns. In this section we shall speak only of nouns as objects.

IN ENGLISH

When a sentence has both a direct and an indirect object, the following two word orders are possible:

1. subject (S) + verb (V) + indirect object (IO) + direct object (DO)

---

[1]In English "to Paul and Mary" is called a **PREPOSITIONAL PHRASE** because it is a phrase that begins with the preposition *to*; in this book we refer to noun and pronoun objects of the preposition *to* as indirect objects since that is how they function in Spanish.

John gave his sister a gift.
| | | |
S   V   IO   DO

Who gave a gift? John.
John is the subject.

John gave *what?* A gift.
A gift is the direct object.

John gave a gift *to whom?* His sister.
His sister is the indirect object.

2. subject + verb + direct object + *to* + indirect object

John gave a gift to his sister.
| | | |
S   V   DO   IO

The first structure, under 1, is the most common. However, because there is no *"to"* preceding the indirect object, it is more difficult to identify its function than in the second structure.

Regardless of the word order, the function of the words in these two sentences is the same because they answer the same question. Be sure to ask the questions to establish the function of words in a sentence.

IN SPANISH

Unlike English, when a sentence has both a direct and an indirect object noun, there is only one word order possible (structure 2): subject + **le** or **les** + verb + direct object + **a** *(to)* + indirect object.

Juan le dio **un regalo a su hermana.**
| | | | | |
S   **le**   V   DO   **a**   IO

(word-for-word: *John **(to her)** gave a gift **to his sister***)

*John gave **his sister a gift.***
*John gave **a gift to his sister.***

OBJECT OF A PREPOSITION
IN ENGLISH

An object of a preposition is a noun or pronoun that follows a preposition and is related to it. It answers the question *whom?* or *what?* asked after the preposition.

John is leaving *with Mary.*
   John is leaving *with whom?* With Mary.
   Mary is the object of the preposition *with.*

The baby eats *with a spoon.*
   The baby eats *with what?* With a spoon.
   A spoon is the object of the preposition *with.*

120

130

140

150

IN SPANISH

As in English, an object of a preposition is a noun or pronoun that follows a preposition and is related to it. It answers the question **¿quién?** or **¿qué?** asked after the preposition.

> Pablo sale **con María**.
> *Paul is leaving **with Mary**.*

> Juan trabaja **para el Sr. Jones**.
> *John works **for Mr. Jones**.*

RELATIONSHIP OF A VERB TO ITS OBJECT

The relationship between a verb and its object is often different in English and Spanish. For example, a verb may take an object of a preposition in English but a direct object in Spanish. Therefore, when you learn a Spanish verb, it is important to find out if it is followed by a preposition and, if so, which one. Your textbook, as well as dictionaries, will indicate when a Spanish verb needs a preposition before an object.

Here are differences you are likely to encounter.

1. ENGLISH: object of a preposition → SPANISH: direct object

> *I am looking **for the book**.*
> > FUNCTION IN ENGLISH: object of a preposition
> > I am looking *for what?* The book.
> > *The book* is the object of the preposition *for*.
> Busco **el libro**.
> > FUNCTION IN SPANISH: direct object
> > **¿Qué busco? El libro.**
> > Since **buscar** *(to look for)* is not followed by a preposition, it takes a direct object.

Many common verbs require an object of a preposition in English, but a direct object in Spanish.

*to look **for***	buscar
*to look **at***	mirar
*to ask **for***	pedir
*to listen **to***	escuchar
*to wait **for***	esperar
*to wait **on***	servir

2. ENGLISH: direct object → SPANISH: object of a preposition

> *John remembers **his apartment** in Madrid.*
> > FUNCTION IN ENGLISH: direct object
> > John remember *what?* His apartment.
> > *His apartment* is the direct object.

Juan se acuerda **de su apartamento** en Madrid. 200
FUNCTION IN SPANISH: object of a preposition
¿**De qué** se acuerda Juan? De su apartamento.
(word-for-word: *of what does John remember? of his apartment*)
Su apartamento is the object of the preposition **de** *(of)*.

A few common verbs require a direct object in English but an object of a preposition in Spanish.

to enjoy	gozar **de**
to enter	entrar **en**
to forget	olvidarse **de**
to leave	salir **de**	210
to marry	casarse **con**
to play	jugar **a**
to remember	acordarse **de**

CAREFUL — Always identify the function of a word within the language in which you are working; do not mix English and Spanish patterns.

SUMMARY

Your ability to recognize the three types of objects is essential. A different Spanish pronoun is used for the English pronoun *him* depending on whether *him* is a direct object (**lo**), 220
an indirect object (**le**), or an object of a preposition (**él**).

The different types of objects in a sentence can be identified by establishing whether they answer a question which requires a preposition or not and, if so, which one.

DIRECT OBJECT — An object that receives the action of the verb directly.

INDIRECT OBJECT — An object that receives the action of the verb indirectly, sometimes with the preposition *to*. 230

OBJECT OF A PREPOSITION — An object that follows a preposition and is related to it.

CHAPTER

40

WHAT ARE DIRECT OBJECT PRONOUNS?

A **DIRECT OBJECT PRONOUN** is used in place of a direct object noun. It receives the action of the verb directly, without a preposition between the verb and the object. It answers the question *whom?* or *what?* asked after the verb (see *What is a Pronoun?*, p. 30 and *What are Objects?*, p. 138).

> Paul saw *her*.
> > Paul saw whom? Answer: Her.
> > *Her* is the direct object of the verb *saw*.

IN ENGLISH

The direct object pronouns are different from the subject pronouns.

	SUBJECT PRONOUNS	DIRECT OBJECT PRONOUNS
SINGULAR		
1ST PERSON	I	me
2ND PERSON	you	you
3RD PERSON	he	him
	she	her
	it	it
PLURAL		
1ST PERSON	we	us
2ND PERSON	you	you
3RD PERSON	they	them

Let us look at a few examples.

> They saw *me*.
> subject direct object
> pronoun pronoun

> She is watching *us*.
> subject direct object
> pronoun pronoun

As you can see, the direct object pronoun is always placed after the verb.

IN SPANISH

As in English, the pronouns used as direct objects are different from the ones used as subjects. Unlike English, however, the form of the object pronoun often changes depending on whether it is a direct or an indirect object.

To choose the correct form here are the steps to follow:

1. Establish if the Spanish verb takes a direct or indirect object (see *Relationship of a verb to its object*, pp. 142-3). 40

   ▪ If the Spanish verb takes a direct object, continue with this chapter.

   ▪ If the Spanish verb takes an indirect object, go to the following chapter to learn the forms of indirect object pronouns *(What are Indirect Object Pronouns?*, p. 148).

2. Depending on the pronoun, follow the steps outlined under the examples below. Since the pattern of the Spanish direct object pronouns for *me, you, him, her, us* is different from the pattern for *it, them, you,* we have divided them into these two categories. 50

Unlike English where the direct object pronouns are placed after the verb, Spanish direct object pronouns are usually placed before the verb. Consult your textbook to learn more about the placement of direct object pronouns in Spanish.

Here are some examples with the verb **ver** *to see* (both the Spanish and the English verbs take an direct object).

Me, you *(tú* and *vosotros* forms), **him, her, us**
The direct object pronouns corresponding to *me, you,* 60
him, her, and *us* have a word-for-word Spanish equivalent. Just select the form you need from the chart below.

DIRECT OBJECTS	
me	me
you [tú form]	te
you [vosotros form]	os
him	lo
her	la
us	nos

*John sees **me.*** 70
    1. IDENTIFY THE VERB: *to see* (**ver**)
    2. FUNCTION OF THE OBJECT: direct object
    3. IDENTIFY THE PRONOUN: *me*
    4. SELECTION: **me**
Juan **me** ve.

*John sees **you.***
Juan **te** ve. [tú form]
Juan **os** ve. [vosotros form]

*Do you see John? Yes, I see **him.***
¿Ves a Juan? Sí, **lo** veo.

*Do you see Mary? Yes, I see **her.***
¿Ves a María? Sí, **la** veo.

*John sees **us.***
Juan **nos** ve.

It, them, you *(usted* and *ustedes* forms)
The direct object pronouns equivalent to *it, them* and *you*
change depending on the gender of the ANTECEDENT; that is,
the noun which they are replacing.

	DIRECT OBJECTS	
	MASCULINE	FEMININE
it	lo	la
you [usted form]	lo	la
them	los	las
you [ustedes form]	los	las

*Does John see the book? Yes, John sees **it.***
    1. IDENTIFY THE VERB: *to see* (**ver**)
    2. FUNCTION OF THE OBJECT: direct object
    3. IDENTIFY THE PRONOUN: *it*
    4. ANTECEDENT: **el libro** *(book)*
    5. GENDER OF ANTECEDENT: masculine
    6. SELECTION: **lo**
¿Ve Juan el libro? Sí, Juan **lo** ve.

*Does John see the table? Yes, John sees **it.***
    4. ANTECEDENT: **la mesa** *(table)*
    5. GENDER OF ANTECEDENT: feminine
    6. SELECTION: **la**
¿Ve Juan la mesa? Sí, Juan **la** ve.

*Does John see the cars? Yes, John sees **them.***
    4. ANTECEDENT: **los coches** *(cars)*
    5. GENDER OF ANTECEDENT: masculine
    6. SELECTION: **los**
¿Ve Juan los coches? Sí, Juan **los** ve.

The pronoun *you* (formal) changes not only according to the
gender of the person or persons you are addressing, but also
according to whether you are addressing one or more persons.

*Whom does John see? John sees **you.*** [a male]
    1. IDENTIFY THE VERB: *to see* (**ver**)
    2. FUNCTION OF THE OBJECT: direct object
    3. IDENTIFY THE PRONOUN: *you*
    4. NUMBER & GENDER OF *YOU:* masculine singular
    5. SELECTION: **lo**
¿A quién ve Juan? Juan **lo** ve.

Whom does John see? John sees you. [a female]
    4. NUMBER & GENDER OF *YOU:* feminine singular
    5. SELECTION: **la**
¿A quién ve Juan? Juan **la** ve.

Whom does John see? John sees you. [males or a mixed group]
    4. NUMBER & GENDER OF *YOU:* masculine plural
    5. SELECTION: **los**
¿A quién ve Juan? Juan **los** ve.

130

Whom does John see? John sees you. [females]
    4. NUMBER & GENDER OF *YOU:* feminine plural
    5. SELECTION: **las**
¿A quién ve Juan? Juan **las** ve.

STUDY TIPS — DIRECT OBJECT PRONOUNS

Pattern (see *Tips for Learning Word Forms*, p. 5)

1. Look for similarities between direct object pronouns and other parts of speech.
   What similarities can you think of?
   - 1st pers. sing. & pl. and 2nd pers. sing. (**me, te, nos**): initial letters **m-, t-, n-** are the same as possessive adjectives (**mi, tu, nuestro**)
   - 3rd pers. fem. sing. & pl. and 3rd pers. masc. pl. (**la, las, los**): same as definite articles (**la, las, los**)

Flashcards

On the subject pronoun flashcards, add sentences illustrating the pronoun's form as direct object.

ella	*she* (subject)
La veo.	*I see **her**.* (direct object)
ellos	*they* (subject, males or mixed group)
Los veo.	*I see **them**.* (direct object)

Practice

1. Since function determines a pronoun's form, it is important to learn direct object pronouns in a sentence.

2. Write a series of short Spanish sentences with masculine and feminine singular and plural nouns as direct objects. Rewrite the sentences replacing the direct object noun with the appropriate direct object pronoun.

Juan ve a Susana.	*John sees Susana.*
Juan **la** ve.	*John sees **her**.*

CHAPTER

WHAT ARE INDIRECT OBJECT PRONOUNS?

1 An **INDIRECT OBJECT PRONOUN** is used in place of an indirect object noun. It receives the action of the verb indirectly and answers the question *to whom?* or *to what?* asked after the verb (see *What is a Pronoun?*, p. 30 and *What are Objects?*, p. 138).

> Paul wrote *to her.*
> Paul wrote to whom? ANSWER: Her.
> *Her* is the indiret object of the verb *wrote.*

IN ENGLISH

10 The indirect object pronouns are different from subject pronouns, but the same pronouns are used as direct objects and indirect objects (see *What are Direct Object Pronouns?*, p. 144).

	SUBJECT PRONOUNS	INDIRECT OBJECT PRONOUNS
SINGULAR		
1ST PERSON	I	me
2ND PERSON	you	you
3RD PERSON	he	him
	she	her
	it	it
PLURAL		
1ST PERSON	we	us
2ND PERSON	you	you
3RD PERSON	they	them

Let us look at a few examples.

> He lent *her* the car.
> subject — indirect object
> pronoun   pronoun

> They gave *me* a birthday present.
> subject — indirect object
> pronoun   pronoun

As you can see, the indirect object pronoun is always placed after the verb.

IN SPANISH

As in English, pronouns used as indirect objects are different from the ones used as subjects. Unlike English, however, the form of the object pronoun often changes depending on whether it is a direct or an indirect object.

To choose the correct form here are the steps to follow:

1. Establish if the Spanish verb takes a direct or indirect object (see *Relationship of a verb to its object*, pp. 142-3).
   - If the Spanish verb takes a direct object, go to the previous chapter to learn the forms of the direct object pronouns *(What are Direct Object Pronouns?*, p. 144).
   - If the Spanish verb takes an indirect object continue with this chapter.
2. Depending on the pronoun, follow the steps outlined under the examples below. Since the pattern of the Spanish indirect object pronouns for *me, you, us* is different from the pattern for *him, her, you, them*, we have divided them into these two categories.

Unlike English where the indirect object pronouns are placed after the verb, Spanish indirect object pronouns are usually placed before the verb. Consult your textbook to learn more about the placement of indirect object pronouns in Spanish.

Here are some examples with the verb **hablar** *to speak* (both the Spanish and the English verbs take an indirect object).

Me, you *(tú* and *vosotros* forms) **us**

The indirect object pronouns corresponding to *me, you,* and *us* are the same as the Spanish direct object pronouns.

INDIRECT OBJECTS	
me	**me**
you [tú form]	**te**
you [vosotros form]	**os**
us	**nos**

*John speaks **to me**.*

    1. IDENTIFY THE VERB: *to speak* (**hablar**)

    2. FUNCTION OF THE OBJECT: indirect object

    3. IDENTIFY THE PRONOUN: *me*

    4. SELECTION: **me**

Juan **me** habla.
    |
    indirect object pronoun

John speaks to you.
Juan **te** habla. [**tú** form]
Juan **os** habla. [**vosotros** form]

John speaks to us.
Juan **nos** habla.

Him, her, you *(usted* and *ustedes* forms)**, them**
The indirect object pronouns equivalent to *him, her, you,*
and *them* do not distinguish between gender; you can just
select the form you need from the chart below.

INDIRECT OBJECTS	
him, her, you [usted form]	**le**
them, you [ustedes form]	**les**

To whom is John speaking? John is speaking to him.
1. IDENTIFY THE VERB: *to speak* (**hablar**)
2. FUNCTION OF THE OBJECT: indirect object
3. IDENTIFY THE PRONOUN: *him*
4. SELECTION: **le**
¿A quién **le** habla Juan? Juan **le** habla.[1]

To whom is John speaking? John is speaking to her.
¿A quién **le** habla Juan? Juan **le** habla.

To whom is John speaking? John is speaking to you. [one person]
1. IDENTIFY THE VERB: *to speak* (**hablar**)
2. FUNCTION OF THE OBJECT: indirect object
3. IDENTIFY THE PRONOUN: *you*
4. SELECTION: **le**
¿A quién **le** habla Juan? Juan **le** habla.

To whom is John speaking? John is speaking to them.
1. IDENTIFY THE VERB: *to speak* (**hablar**)
2. FUNCTION OF THE OBJECT: indirect object
3. IDENTIFY THE PRONOUN: *them*
4. SELECTION: **les**
¿A quiénes **les** habla Juan? Juan **les** habla.

To whom is John speaking? John is speaking to you. [many persons]
1. IDENTIFY THE VERB: *to speak* (**hablar**)
2. FUNCTION OF THE OBJECT: indirect object
3. IDENTIFY THE PRONOUN: *you*
4. SELECTION: **les**
¿A quiénes **les** habla Juan? Juan **les** habla.

[1]For the inclusion of "**le**" in the question, see p. 140.

In order to distinguish **le** meaning *to him* from **le** meaning *to her* or *to you,* the phrase **a él, a ella,** or **a usted** can be added to the end of the sentence.

Juan **le** habla **a él.**	*John speaks **to him.***
Juan **le** habla **a ella.**	*John speaks **to her.***
Juan **le** habla **a usted.**	*John speaks **to you.***

In order to distinguish **les** meaning *to them* (masculine or feminine) and *to you,* the phrase **a ellos, a ellas,** or **a ustedes** can be added to the end of the sentence.

Juan **les** habla **a ellos.**	*John speaks **to them.*** [to males or to a mixed group]
Juan **les** habla **a ellas.**	*John speaks **to them.*** [to females]
Juan **les** habla **a ustedes.**	*John speaks **to you.***

SPANISH USE OF INDIRECT OBJECT PRONOUNS IN PLACE OF SUBJECT PRONOUNS

In Spanish there are a number of common verbs that use an indirect object pronoun where English uses a subject pronoun. Look at the following examples with the verb **gustar** *to like.*

subject   direct object

I like that jacket.

Me gusta esa **chaqueta.**
to me is pleasing that jacket

indirect object   subject

subject   direct object

He likes that book.

Le gusta ese **libro.**
to him is pleasing that book

indirect object   subject

Consult your textbook for a more detailed explanation of verbs that function like **gustar** and that use an indirect object pronoun where English uses a subject.

SUMMARY

To distinguish Spanish direct object pronouns from Spanish indirect object pronouns, be aware that:

- the following Spanish object pronouns have the same form when used as direct and indirect objects.

DIRECT AND INDIRECT OBJECTS	
me	me
you [tú form]	te
you [vosotros form]	os
we	nos

- the following Spanish object pronouns have different forms when used as direct and indirect objects.

	DIRECT OBJECTS	INDIRECT OBJECTS
him	lo	le
her	la	le
it	lo, la	le
you [usted form]	lo, la	le
them	los, las	les
you [ustedes form]	los, las	les

- the following Spanish direct object pronouns have a different form depending on the gender of the antecedent.

	DIRECT OBJECTS	
	MASCULINE	FEMININE
it	lo	la
you [usted form]	lo	la
them	los	las
you [ustedes form]	los	las

STUDY TIPS — INDIRECT OBJECT PRONOUNS

Pattern (see *Tips for Learning Word Forms,* p. 5)

When you learn indirect object pronouns, look for similarities with direct object pronouns as well as other parts of speech.

What similarities do you notice?

- 1st, 2nd pers. sing. & pl. (**me, te, nos, os**): same forms for direct and indirect object pronouns
- 3rd pers. sing. & pl. (**le, les**): same forms for masculine and feminine
- 3rd pers. sing. & pl. (**lo, la, las, los, le, les**): all begin with letter **l-**

Flashcards

On the subject pronoun flashcards, add sentences illustrating the pronoun's form as indirect object.

ella	*she* (subject)
Le hablo.	*I speak **to her**.* (indirect object)
ellos	*they* (subject, males or mixed group)
Les hablo.	*I speak **to them**.* (indirect object)

Practice

1. Since function determines a pronoun's form, it is important to learn indirect object pronouns in a sentence.

2. Write a series of short Spanish sentences with nouns as indirect objects. Rewrite the sentences replacing the indirect object noun with the appropriate indirect object pronoun.

Juan le da un regalo a Susana.	*John gives a gift to Susan.*
Juan **le** da un regalo.	*John gives **her** a gift.*

CHAPTER

WHAT ARE OBJECT OF PREPOSITION PRONOUNS?

1 An OBJECT OF A PREPOSITION pronoun follows a preposition and is related to it. It answers the question *whom?* or *what?* asked after the preposition.

> They went out with *me.*
> They went out with whom? Answer: With *me.*
> *Me* is the object of preposition pronoun.

IN ENGLISH

The same forms of object pronouns are used for direct object pronouns, indirect object pronouns, and object of
10 preposition pronouns (see *What are Direct Object Pronouns?*, p. 144 and *What are Indirect Object Pronouns?*, p. 148).

IN SPANISH

Pronouns that are objects of a preposition other than the preposition *to* have forms that are different from the forms used as direct object pronouns and indirect object pronouns.

Let us look at the Spanish object of preposition pronouns to see how they are selected. First, you have to
20 establish that in Spanish there is a preposition, and if so, which one. Remember that English and Spanish verbs do not always use the same preposition, if any, and that when working in Spanish you have to establish the preposition used in Spanish. As in English, object of preposition pronouns are always placed after the preposition.

To simplify our examples in this section we have chosen English and Spanish verbs that take the same preposition.

Since the pattern of object of preposition pronouns for *me, you* (**tú, usted** and **ustedes** forms), *him,* and *her* is dif-
30 ferent from the pattern for *us, you* (**vosotros** form), and *them,* we have divided the Spanish object of preposition pronouns into these two categories.

Me, you (*tú, usted, ustedes* forms), **him, her**
The object of preposition pronouns corresponding to *me, you, him,* and *her* have a word-for-word Spanish equivalent. Just select the form you need from the following chart.

OBJECTS OF A PREPOSITION	
me	**mí**
you [tú form]	**ti**
him	**él**
her	**ella**
you [usted form]	**usted**
you [ustedes form]	**ustedes**

40

Here are some examples.

*Is the book for John? No, it's **for me.***
    1. IDENTIFY THE PREPOSITION: *for*
    2. IDENTIFY THE OBJECT OF THE PREPOSITION: *me*
    3. SELECTION: **mí**
¿Es para Juan el libro? No, es **para mí.**

50

*Is the book for John? Yes, it is **for him.***
    1. IDENTIFY THE PREPOSITION: *for*
    2. IDENTIFY THE OBJECT OF THE PREPOSITION: *him*
    3. SELECTION: **él**
¿Es para Juan el libro? Sí, es **para él.**

*Is the book for Mary? Yes, it is **for her.***
    1. IDENTIFY THE PREPOSITION: *for*
    2. IDENTIFY THE OBJECT OF THE PREPOSITION: *her*
    3. SELECTION: **ella**
¿Es para María el libro? Sí, es **para ella.**

60

*Is the book for John? No, it's **for you.*** [one person]
    1. IDENTIFY THE PREPOSITION: *for*
    2. IDENTIFY THE OBJECT OF THE PREPOSITION: *you*
    3. DISTINGUISH FORMAL FROM FAMILIAR: familiar
    4. NUMBER OF THE PRONOUN *you*: singular
    5. SELECTION: **ti**
¿Es para Juan el libro? No, es **para ti.**

*Is the book for me? Yes, it is **for you.*** [one person]
    1. IDENTIFY THE PREPOSITION: *for*
    2. IDENTIFY THE OBJECT OF THE PREPOSITION: *you*
    3. DISTINGUISH FORMAL FROM FAMILIAR: formal

70

    4. NUMBER OF THE PRONOUN *you*: singular
    5. SELECTION: **usted**
¿Es para mí el libro? Sí, es **para usted.**

*Are the books for us? Yes, they're **for you.*** [more than one person]
    1. IDENTIFY THE PREPOSITION: *for*
    2. IDENTIFY THE OBJECT OF THE PREPOSITION: *you*
    3. DISTINGUISH FORMAL FROM FAMILIAR: formal
    4. NUMBER OF THE PRONOUN *you*: plural
    5. SELECTION: **ustedes**
¿Son para nosotros los libros? Sí, son **para ustedes.**

Us, you *(vosotros* form), **them**
The object of preposition pronouns equivalent to *us, you,*
and *them* change depending on the gender of the persons
they refer to.

OBJECTS OF A PREPOSITION		
	MASCULINE	FEMININE
us	**nosotros**	**nosotras**
you	**vosotros**	**vosotras**
them	**ellos**	**ellas**

*Are the books for John? No, they're **for us.*** [group of males or mixed group]
    1. IDENTIFY THE PREPOSITION: *for*
    2. IDENTIFY THE OBJECT OF THE PREPOSITION: *us*
    3. GENDER OF THE PRONOUN *US*: masculine
    4. SELECTION: **nosotros**
¿Son para Juan los libros? No, son **para nosotros.**

*Are the books for John? No, they're **for us.*** [group of females]
    1. - 2. (see above)
    3. GENDER OF THE PRONOUN *US*: feminine
    4. SELECTION: **nosotras**
¿Son para Juan los libros? No, son **para nosotras.**

*Are the books for John? No, they're **for you.*** [group of males or mixed group]
    1. IDENTIFY THE PREPOSITION: *for*
    2. IDENTIFY THE OBJECT OF THE PREPOSITION: *you*
    3. DISTINGUISH FORMAL FROM FAMILIAR: familiar
    4. NUMBER OF THE PRONOUN *YOU*: plural
    5. GENDER OF THE PRONOUN *YOU*: masculine
    6. SELECTION: **vosotros**
¿Son para Juan los libros? No, son **para vosotros.**

*Are the books for John? No, they're **for you.*** [group of females]
    1. - 4. (see above)
    5. GENDER OF THE PRONOUN *YOU*: feminine
    6. SELECTION: **vosotras**
¿Son para Juan los libros? No, son **para vosotras.**

*Is the book for the children? Yes, it's **for them.***
    1. IDENTIFY THE PREPOSITION: *for*
    2. IDENTIFY THE OBJECT OF THE PREPOSITION: *them*
    3. GENDER OF THE PRONOUN *THEM*: masculine *(boys)*
    4. SELECTION: **ellos**
¿Es para los niños el libro? Sí, es **para ellos.**

*Is the book for Mary and Gloria? Yes, it's **for them.***
  1. - 2. (see above)
  3. GENDER OF THE PRONOUN *THEM*: feminine *(Mary and Gloria)*
  4. SELECTION: **ellas**
¿Es para María y Gloria el libro? Sí, es **para ellas.**

CAREFUL — The English object of preposition pronouns for *it* or *them* referring to things has no Spanish equivalent

STUDY TIPS — OBJECT OF PREPOSITION PRONOUNS

Pattern
1. The 1st pers. sing. form has a written accent mark, **mí**.
2. Look for similarities between object of preposition pronouns (charts on p. 155 and p. 156) and other parts of speech with 1st, 2nd and 3rd persons that you've already learned.

	OBJ. OF PREP. PRONOUNS	SUBJECT PRONOUNS	POSSESSIVE ADJECTIVES SING.
SINGULAR			
1st pers.	mí	yo	mi
2nd pers.	ti	tú	tu
3rd pers.	él / ella / usted	él / ella / usted	su
PLURAL			
1st pers.	nosotros	nosotros	nuestr-
2nd pers.	vosotros	vosotros	vuestr-
3rd pers.	ellos / ellas / ustedes	ellos / ellas / ustedes	su

What similarities do you notice between object of preposition pronouns and the other parts of speech above?
- all forms except 1st and 2nd pers. sing.: same as subject pronouns
- 1st pers. sing.: only an accent distinguishes the possessive adjective **mi** from the object pronoun **mí**
- 1st pers. pl. and 2nd per. sing. & pl.: initial letter same as initial letter of subject pronoun and possessive adjectives: 1st pers. pl. **n-**, 2nd pers. sing. **t-**, 2nd pers. pl. **v-**

Flashcards
On the subject pronoun flashcards, add sentences illustrating the object of preposition forms.

yo	*I*
Es **para mí.**	*It's **for me.***
ellas	*them* (group of females)
Es **para ellas.**	*It's **for them.***

Practice

Create Spanish sentences with a noun object of a preposition. Then, replace the noun with the pronoun.

El regalo es para María.	*The gift is for Mary.*
El regalo es **para ella**.	*The gift is **for her**.*
Carlos vive cerca de Juan.	*Charles lives near John.*
Carlos vive **cerca de él**.	*Charles lives **near him**.*

WHAT ARE REFLEXIVE PRONOUNS AND VERBS?

A **REFLEXIVE VERB** is a verb which is accompanied by a pronoun, called a **REFLEXIVE PRONOUN**, that serves "to reflect" the action of the verb back to the subject.

1

subject = reflexive pronoun → the same person

She *cut herself* with the knife.

reflexive verb

IN ENGLISH

Many regular verbs can take on a reflexive meaning by adding a reflexive pronoun.

10

The child *dresses* the doll.

regular verb

The child *dresses herself.*

verb + reflexive pronoun

Reflexive pronouns end with *-self* in the singular and *-selves* in the plural.

	SUBJECT PRONOUN	REFLEXIVE PRONOUN
SINGULAR		
1ˢᵀ PERSON	I	myself
2ᴺᴰ PERSON	you	yourself
3ᴿᴰ PERSON	he	himself
	she	herself
	it	itself
PLURAL		
1ˢᵀ PERSON	we	ourselves
2ᴺᴰ PERSON	you	yourselves
3ᴿᴰ PERSON	they	themselves

20
30

As the subject changes so does the reflexive pronoun, because they both refer to the same person or object.

I cut *myself.*
John and Mary blamed *themselves* for the accident.

Although the subject pronoun *you* is the same for the singular and plural, there is a difference in the reflexive pronouns: *yourself* (singular) is used when you are speaking to one person and *yourselves* (plural) is used when you are speaking to more than one.

> *Paul*, did *you* make *yourself* a sandwich?
> *Children*, make sure *you* wash *yourselves* properly.

Reflexive verbs can be in any tense: *I wash myself, I washed myself, I will wash myself,* etc.

IN SPANISH

As in English, Spanish reflexive verbs are formed with a verb and a reflexive pronoun.

Here are the Spanish reflexive pronouns:

SINGULAR

1ST PERSON	me	*myself*
2ND PERSON	te	*yourself* [**tú** form]
3RD PERSON	se	*himself, herself, yourself* [**usted** form]

PLURAL

1ST PERSON	nos	*ourselves*
2ND PERSON	os	*yourselves* [**vosotros** form]
3RD PERSON	se	*themselves, yourselves* [**ustedes** form]

In the dictionary, reflexive verbs are listed under the regular verb. For instance, under **lavar** *(to wash)* you will also find **lavarse** *(to wash oneself)*. Notice that the reflexive pronoun **se** is attached to the end of the infinitive to indicate a reflexive verb.

Look at the conjugation of **lavarse**. Notice two things:

1. as in English, the reflexive pronoun changes according to the person of the conjugation
2. unlike English, the reflexive pronoun is placed before the conjugated verb

	SUBJECT PRONOUN	+ REFLEXIVE PRONOUN +	VERB
SINGULAR			
1ST PERSON	yo	me	lavo
2ND PERSON	tú	te	lavas
3RD PERSON	él / ella / usted	se	lava

PLURAL

1ˢᵀ PERSON	{ nosotros nosotras }	nos	lavamos
2ⁿᵈ PERSON	{ vosotros vosotras }	os	laváis
3ᴿᴰ PERSON	{ ellos ellas ustedes }	se	lavan

80

Reflexive verbs can be conjugated in all tenses. The subject pronoun and reflexive pronoun remain the same regardless of the tense of the verb, only the verb form changes: **él se lavará** (future); **él se lavó** (preterite).

Reflexive verbs are common in Spanish. There are many expressions that are not reflexive in English, but whose Spanish equivalent is a reflexive verb. You will have to memorize such expressions individually.

90

to wake up	despertarse *(to wake oneself up)*
to get up	levantarse *(to get oneself up)*
to go to bed	acostarse *(to put oneself to bed)*
to go to sleep	dormirse *(to put oneself to sleep)*
to get dressed	vestirse *(to dress oneself)*
to have a good time	divertirse *(to amuse oneself)*
to be worried	preocuparse *(to worry oneself)*

In all the examples above, the Spanish reflexive pronouns have a meaning equivalent to the English reflexive pronouns listed on p. 159 *(myself, yourself, himself,* etc.). This is not always the case. Sometimes the addition of a reflexive pronoun will change the meaning of a verb as in the following example: **ir** → *to go*; **irse** → *to go away*. As you will see below, Spanish reflexive pronouns can also indicate reciprocal action.

100

RECIPROCAL ACTION

IN ENGLISH

110

To express reciprocal action, that is, an action between two or more persons or things, English uses a regular verb followed by the expression "each other."

The dog and the cat looked at *each other.*

> The expression "each other" tells us that the action of "looking" was reciprocal, i.e. the dog looked at the cat and the cat looked at the dog.

Our children call *each other* every day.

120
The expression "each other" tells us that the action of "calling" is reciprocal, i.e. the various children call one another every day.

Reciprocal verbs are always plural since they require that more than one person or thing be involved.

IN SPANISH

Spanish uses reflexive pronouns to express an action that is reciprocal.

El perro y el gato **se** miraron.
*The dog and the cat looked at **each other**.*

130
Nuestros hijos **se** llaman cada día.
*Our children call **each other** every day.*

Context will often indicate if the meaning of the Spanish pronoun is reflexive *(-self, -selves)* or reciprocal *(each other)*.

Las chicas **se** miran en el espejo.
The information "en el espejo" *(in the mirror)* leads us to believe that the girls are looking at themselves. Therefore, **se** is reflexive.
*The girls look at **themselves** in the mirror.*
|
reflexive

140
However, when no information is given, the meaning of the Spanish sentence is ambiguous.

Las chicas **se miran**.
*The girls **look at themselves**.*   →   REFLEXIVE
*The girls **look at each other**.*   →   RECIPROCAL

One way to avoid ambiguity, and to indicate that the meaning is reciprocal rather than reflexive, is to add an expression equivalent to "each other," such as "**el uno al otro**" (singular) or "**los unos a los otros**" (plural).

150
El perro y el gato **se** miran **el uno al otro**.
    | | |_____|
   masc. sing.   masc. sing.   masc. sing.
*The dog and the cat look at **each other**.*

Los niños **se** miran **los unos a los otros**.
    | |_____|
   masc. pl.   masc. pl.
*The children look at **each other**.*

Consult your textbook for detailed explanations.

WHAT IS A POSSESSIVE PRONOUN?

A **POSSESSIVE PRONOUN** is a word that replaces a noun and ind-   1
cates the possessor of that noun. The word *possessive* comes
from *possess,* to own.

> Whose house is that? It's *mine.*
>
> replaces the noun *house,* the object possessed,
> and shows who possesses it, *me*

IN ENGLISH

Here is a list of the possessive pronouns:

SINGULAR POSSESSOR

1ST PERSON		mine
2ND PERSON		yours
3RD PERSON	{ MASCULINE	his
	FEMININE	hers

10

PLURAL POSSESSOR

1ST PERSON	ours
2ND PERSON	yours
3RD PERSON	theirs

Possessive pronouns only refer to the possessor, not to the
object possessed.

20

> My car is red; what color is John's? *His* is blue.
>
> 3rd pers. masc. sing.

> John's car is blue. What color is yours? *Mine* is white.
>
> 1st pers. sing.

> Although the object possessed is the same *(car),* different
> possessive pronouns *(his* and *mine)* are used because the
> possessors are different *(John* and *me).*

> Is that John's house? Yes, it is *his.*
> Are those John's keys? Yes, they are *his.*

30

> Although the objects possessed are different *(house* and
> *keys),* the same possessive pronoun *(his)* is used because
> the possessor is the same *(John).*

IN SPANISH

Like English, Spanish possessive pronouns refer to the possessor. Unlike English, and like all Spanish pronouns, they
also agree in gender and number with the **ANTECEDENT,**

that is, with the person or object possessed. In addition, possessive pronouns are preceded by the definite article that agrees in gender and number with the antecedent.

Let us look at some English sentences to see how to analyze them in order to find the correct form of the Spanish possessive pronoun.

*Where are your books? **Mine** are in the living room.*

1. Find the possessor (*mine* → 1ˢᵗ person singular).
2. Find the antecedent (*mine* refers to *books*).
3. Establish the gender and number of the Spanish equivalent of the antecedent (*books*).
4. Choose the ending of the possessive pronoun that corresponds in gender and number to step 3 above.
5. Choose the definite article that corresponds in gender and number to step 3 above.

¿Dónde están tus libros? **Los míos** están en la sala.

1. The 1ˢᵗ person singular possessor *(mine)* is indicated by the first two letters of the 1ˢᵗ person singular possessive pronoun → **mí-**.
2. The antecedent is **libros** *(books)*.
3. **Libros** is masculine plural.
4. The masculine plural ending is **-os**.
5. The masculine plural definite article is **los**.

Let us look at the Spanish possessive pronouns to learn how to form them. Each possessive pronoun has four forms depending on the gender and number of the antecedent. To choose the proper form follow these steps.

1. Indicate the possessor. This will be shown by the first letters of the possessive pronoun. They are the same initial letters as the stressed possessive adjectives (see *What is a Possessive Adjective?*, p. 117).

Sɪɴɢᴜʟᴀʀ ᴘᴏssᴇssᴏʀ

1ˢᵗ PERSON		mine	**mí-**
2ᴺᴰ PERSON		yours	**tuy-**
3ᴿᴰ PERSON	MASCULINE	his	
	FEMININE	hers	**suy-**
		yours	

Pʟᴜʀᴀʟ ᴘᴏssᴇssᴏʀ

1ˢᵗ PERSON	ours	**nuestr-**
2ᴺᴰ PERSON	yours	**vuestr-**
3ᴿᴰ PERSON	theirs	**suy-**
	yours	

2. Establish the gender and number of the antecedent and choose the definite article and the ending that corresponds to its gender and number. 80

- antecedent is masculine singular → **el** + first letters of the possessor + **-o**

¿Dónde está **el libro?**	El **mío** está en la mesa.
masculine singular	El **tuyo** está en la mesa.
	El **suyo** está en la mesa.
	El **nuestro** está en la mesa.
	El **vuestro** está en la mesa.
	El **suyo** está en la mesa.
*Where is **the book?***	*Mine is on the table.*
	Yours is on the table. 90
	His (hers, yours) is on the table.
	Ours is on the table.
	Yours is on the table.
	Theirs (yours) is on the table.

- antecedent is feminine singular → **la** + first letters of the possessor + **-a**

¿Dónde está **la revista?**	La **mía** está en la mesa.
feminine singular	La **tuya** está en la mesa.
	La **suya** está en la mesa.
	La **nuestra** está en la mesa.
	La **vuestra** está en la mesa. 100
	La **suya** está en la mesa.
*Where is **the magazine?***	*Mine is on the table.*
	Yours is on the table.
	His (hers, yours) is on the table.
	Ours is on the table.
	Yours is on the table.
	Theirs (yours) is on the table.

- antecedent is masculine plural → **los** + first letters of the possessor + **-os**

¿Dónde están **los libros?**	Los **míos** están en la mesa. 110
masculine plural	Los **tuyos** están en la mesa.
	Los **suyos** están en la mesa.
	Los **nuestros** están en la mesa.
	Los **vuestros** están en la mesa.
	Los **suyos** están en la mesa.
*Where are **the books?***	*Mine are on the table.*
	Yours are on the table.
	His (hers, yours) are on the table.
	Ours are on the table.
	Yours are on the table.
	Theirs (yours) are on the table.

- antecedent is feminine plural → **las** + first letters of the possessor + **-as**

¿Dónde están **las revistas?** **Las mías** están en la mesa.
feminine plural **Las tuyas** están en la mesa.
Las suyas están en la mesa.
Las nuestras están en la mesa.
Las vuestras están en la mesa.
Las suyas están en la mesa.

*Where are **the magazines?*** ***Mine** are on the table.*
***Yours** are on the table.*
His (hers, yours) are on the table.
***Ours** are on the table.*
***Yours** are on the table.*
Theirs (yours) are on the table.

3. Select the proper form according to the two steps above.

Let us apply these steps to some examples.

*Mary forgot her notebook but we have **ours.***
1. POSSESSOR: 1st person plural → **nuestr-**
2. ANTECEDENT: **cuaderno** *(notebook)* → masculine singular
3. SELECTION: **el + nuestr- + -o**

María olvidó su cuaderno pero tenemos **el nuestro.**

*I do not have my books, but John and Mary have **theirs.***
1. POSSESSOR: 3rd person plural → **suy-**
2. ANTECEDENT: **libros** *(books)* → masculine plural
3. SELECTION: **los + suy- + -os**

No tengo mis libros pero Juan y María tienen **los suyos.**

*Mary is reading her magazines. John is reading **his.***
1. POSSESSOR: 3rd person singular → **suy-**
2. ANTECEDENT: **revistas** *(magazines)* → feminine plural
3. SELECTION: **las + suy- + -as**

María lee sus revistas. Juan lee **las suyas.**

CAREFUL — The definite article is not used when the possessive pronoun follows a form of the verb **ser** *(to be).*

*Is this your coat? No, it's not **mine. Mine** is larger.*
¿Es este tu abrigo? No, no es **mío. El mío** es más grande.

possessive pronoun   article + possessive
without article   peonoun
after **ser**

SUMMARY

Here is a chart you can use as a reference.

SINGULAR POSSESSOR		ANTECEDENT	
		SINGULAR	PLURAL
mine	MASC.	el mío	los míos
	FEM.	la mía	las mías
yours [tú form]	MASC.	el tuyo	los tuyos
	FEM.	la tuya	las tuyas
his, hers, yours [Ud. form]	MASC.	el suyo	los suyos
	FEM.	la suya	las suyas
PLURAL POSSESSOR		ANTECEDENT	
		SINGULAR	PLURAL
ours	MASC.	el nuestro	los nuestros
	FEM.	la nuestra	las nuestras
yours [vosotros form]	MASC.	el vuestro	los vuestros
	FEM.	la vuestra	las vuestras
theirs, yours [Uds. form]	MASC.	el suyo	los suyos
	FEM.	la suya	las suyas

160

170

STUDY TIPS — POSSESSIVE PRONOUNS

Pattern

1. It will be easy for you to establish a pattern if you remember that possessive pronouns have the same forms as the stressed possessive adjectives and that they are used with the corresponding definite article (see *What is a Possessive Adjective?*, p. 117).

2. It is the use of the definite article that distinguishes the possessive pronouns from the possessive adjectives.

Flashcards

1. For review, create one card per person (1st, 2nd, 3rd pers. sing. and pl.) with an example of the different forms.

> **el mío**, la mía, los míos, las mías   *mine*

2. On all cards add an example that shows the possessive pronoun without the definite article when it follows the verb **ser** *(to be)*.

> ¿De quién son estos zapatos?   *Whose shoes are these?*
> No, son **míos. Los míos** son rojos. *They're not **mine**. **Mine** are red.*

3. On the cards for the 3rd pers. sing. and pl., to reinforce the fact that **el suyo, la suya, los suyos, las suyas** can mean *his, hers, yours,* and *theirs,* write Spanish questions requiring answers equivalent to *his, hers, yours,* and *theirs.*

> ¿Es el libro de María (Juan)?   *Is it Mary's (John's) book?*
> Sí, es **suyo.**   *Yes, it's **hers (his).***
>
> ¿Son los libros de María (Juan)?   *Are they Mary's (John's) books?*
> Sí, son **suyos.**   *Yes, they're **hers (his).***

Practice

1. Sort out your noun flashcards and select a few masculine and feminine nouns.

2. Look at the Spanish side and go through the cards replacing the nouns with the correct form of the possessive pronoun.

> el coche   *car*
> el mío, el tuyo, el suyo, el nuestro, el vuestro
>
> la casa   *house*
> la mía, la tuya, la suya, la nuestra, la vuestra

3. Write short questions in Spanish requiring an answer with a possessive pronoun.

> ¿Es tu libro?   *Is it your book?*
> Sí, es **mío.**   *Yes, it's **mine.***
>
> ¿Son tus llaves?   *Are they your keys?*
> No, no son **mías.**   *No, they're not **mine.***
> **Las mías** estan en mi cuarto.   *Mine are in my room.*

4. Give negative answers to the questions you wrote under No. 3 above so that the answer will require a different possessive pronoun from the one given above.

> ¿Es tu libro?   *Is it your book?*
> No, es **suyo.**   *No, it's **his (hers, yours, theirs).***
>
> ¿Son tus llaves?   *Are they your keys?*
> No, son **suyas.**   *No, they're **his (hers, yours, theirs)***

WHAT IS AN INTERROGATIVE PRONOUN?

An **INTERROGATIVE PRONOUN** is a word that refers to a noun and introduces a question. The word *interrogative* comes from *interrogate,* to question.

> *Who* is coming for dinner?
>
> refers to a person

> *What* did you eat for dinner?
>
> refers to a thing

In both English and Spanish, a different interrogative pronoun is used depending on its **ANTECEDENT,** i.e.,whether it refers to a "person" (human beings and live animals) or a "thing" (objects and ideas). Also, the form of the interrogative pronoun often changes according to its function in the sentence: subject, direct object, indirect object, and object of a preposition. We shall look at each type separately.

INTERROGATIVE PRONOUNS REFERRING TO A PERSON "WHO, WHOM, WHOSE"
IN ENGLISH

Who is used for the subject of the sentence.

> *Who* lives here?
>
> subject

> *Who* are they?
>
> subject

Whom is used for the direct object, indirect object, and object of a preposition.

> *Whom* do you know here?
>
> direct object

> *To whom* did you speak?
>
> indirect object

> *From whom* did you get the book?
>
> object of preposition *from*

Whose is the possessive form and is used to ask about possession or ownership.

1
10
20
30

There's a pencil on the floor? *Whose* is it?
possessive

They are nice cars. *Whose* are they?
possessive

IN SPANISH

The interrogative pronoun referring to persons is always **quién** or **quiénes** regardless of its function within the sentence. The use of **quién** or **quiénes** depends on the number of its ANTECEDENT.

Who or *whom* → **quién** or **quiénes**

Since there is no English equivalent for **quiénes**, both the singular and plural forms translate as *who* or *whom* in English.

■ a question with **quién** asks for a singular response

¿Quién viene? Juan viene.

singular subject   singular response

Who is coming? John is coming.

■ a question with **quiénes** asks for a plural response

¿Quiénes vienen? Juan, Roberto y Miguel vienen.

plural subject   plural response

Who is coming? John, Robert and Michael are coming.

The two examples below require that you restructure the dangling prepositions (see p. 171).

*Who are you leaving **with**? I'm leaving with Robert.* →
*****With whom** are you leaving? I'm leaving with Robert.*

   singular   singular response

¿Con quién sales? Salgo con Roberto.

*Who are you leaving **with**? I'm leaving with my friends.* →
*****With whom** are you leaving? I'm leaving with my friends.*

   plural   plural response

¿Con quiénes sales? Salgo con mis amigos.

Whose → **de quién** or **de quiénes**

English sentences with *whose* can be reworded in order to establish the correct word order in Spanish.

1. Replace *whose* with "of whom."

2. Invert the word order of the subject and verb, that is place the verb before the subject.

Whose car is that?

(word-for-word: *of whom is that car*)   80
¿**De quién** es ese coche?

DANGLING PREPOSITIONS
(see *What is a Preposition?*, p. 135)
IN ENGLISH

In English it is difficult to identify the function of pronouns that are objects of a preposition because the pronouns are often separated from the preposition. Consequently, in conversation the interrogative subject pronoun *who* is often used instead of the interrogative   90
object pronoun *whom*.

Who did you give the book *to?*

interrogative   dangling preposition
pronoun

When a preposition is separated from its object and placed at the end of a sentence or question, it is called a **DANGLING PREPOSITION.**

To enable you to establish the function of an interrogative pronoun, you will have to change the structure of the sentence so that the preposition is placed before the interrogative pronoun. In formal English there is a tendency to avoid dangling prepositions.   100

SPOKEN ENGLISH   →   **FORMAL ENGLISH**
Who did you speak *to?*   *To whom* did you speak?

instead of *whom*   preposition

Who did you get the book *from?*   *From whom* did you get the book?

instead of *whom*   preposition

IN SPANISH   110

Spanish places prepositions in the same position as formal English; that is, within the sentence or at the beginning of a question. By restructuring English sentences or questions with dangling prepositions you will not only be able to identify the function of interrogative pronouns (and relative pronouns, see p. 182), but also establish the word order for the Spanish sentence.

Here are a few examples of sentences which have been restructured to avoid the dangling preposition.

120

Who are you writing **to**?   → **To whom** are you writing?
    | | |
subject form of   preposition   object form of
interr. pronoun   interr. pronoun

¿A quién le escribes?

Who are you leaving **with**?   → **With whom** are you leaving?
    | | |
subject form of   preposition   object form of
interr. pronoun   interr. pronoun

¿Con quién sales?

Who did you buy the gift **for**? → **For whom** did you buy the gift?
    | | |
130
subject form of   preposition   object form of
interr. pronoun   interr. pronoun

¿Para quién compraste el regalo?

INTERROGATIVE PRONOUN REFERRING TO A THING "WHAT"

IN ENGLISH

What refers only to things or ideas. The same form is used for subject, direct object, indirect object, and the object of a preposition.

140

What happened?
  |
subject

What do you want?
   |
direct object

What is the movie about?
 |
object of preposition *about*

IN SPANISH

150

The interrogative pronoun referring to things is always **qué** regardless of its function within the sentence.

What happened?
¿**Qué** pasó?

What do you want?
¿**Qué** quieres?

What is the movie *about*? → *About what* is the movie?
¿**De qué** trata la película?

INTERROGATIVE PRONOUNS REQUESTING A SELECTION "WHICH ONE, WHICH ONES"

IN ENGLISH

160

Which (one), *which (ones)* are used in questions that request the selection of one *(which one*, singular) or more than one *(which ones*, plural) from a group that has already been mentioned. The words *one* and *ones* are often omitted from the phrase. These interrogative pronouns can refer to both persons and things and they do not change according to their function.

All the teachers are here. *Which (one)* teaches Spanish?
group   singular subject

170

I have two cars. *Which (one)* do you want to take?
group   singular direct object

The library has many books. *Which (ones)* do you want?
group   plural direct object

He has a group of friends. *Which (ones)* does he live with?
group   plural object of preposition *with*

IN SPANISH

As in English these interrogative pronouns do not change according to function. Their form does change, however, according to what you want to say: *which one* (singular) → **cuál** or *which ones* (plural) → **cuáles.**

180

Which one do you need?
¿**Cuál** necesitas?

Which ones do you need?
¿**Cuáles** necesitas?

If the English word *one* or *ones* is not expressed, look at the verb. If the verb is singular, use **cuál**; if the verb is plural, use **cuáles.**

190

Which of the girls is Spanish?
singular verb
¿**Cuál** de las chicas **es** española?

Which of the girls are Spanish?
plural verb
¿**Cuáles** de las chicas **son** españolas?

CAREFUL — *What is, what are* has two equivalents in Spanish: **qué** + **ser** or **cuál(-es)** + **ser**. To determine which to use you need to decide what the expected answer will be.

- expected answer is a definition → **qué** + **ser**

    What is *the Nobel Prize?*
    > The expected answer is a definition of the Nobel Prize.

    ¿Qué es el Premio Nobel?

    What are *the Panamerican Games?*
    > The expected answer is a definition of the Panamerican Games.

    ¿Qué son los Juegos Panamericanos?

- expected answer varies and answers the question *which one(-s)* of many → **cuál(-es)** + **ser**

    What is *your favorite novel?*
    > The expected answer will explain which novel of the many that exist is the favorite.

    ¿Cuál es su novela favorita?

    What are *the countries of Europe?*
    > The expected answer will explain which countries of the many in the world are European.

    ¿Cuáles son los países de Europa?

There is another interrogative pronoun that we will now examine separately since it does not follow the same pattern as above.

"HOW MUCH, HOW MANY"
IN ENGLISH

The English interrogative pronouns ***how much, how many*** are a rare example of English pronouns that change to agree in number with the noun they replace.

I have paper. *How much* do you need?
     singular   singular
     noun   pronoun

I have some pencils. *How many* do you need?
     plural   plural
     noun   pronoun

IN SPANISH

This interrogative pronoun has four forms that change according to the gender and number of the ANTECEDENT, that is, the noun replaced by the pronoun.

240

	SINGULAR *how much*	PLURAL *how many*
MASCULINE	cuánto	cuántos
FEMININE	cuánta	cuántas

To choose the proper form, follow these steps:

1. Determine the antecedent.
2. Determine the gender of the antecedent.
3. Determine the number of the antecedent.

250

Let us apply these steps to some examples.

I have a lot of paper. ***How much** do you want?*
    1. ANTECEDENT: **el papel** *(paper)*
    2. GENDER OF ANTECEDENT: masculine
    3. NUMBER OF ANTECEDENT: singular
    4. SELECTION: **cuánto**
Tengo mucho papel. ¿**Cuánto** quieres?

I have a lot of meat. ***How much** do you want?*
    1. ANTECEDENT: **la carne** *(meat)*
    2. GENDER OF ANTECEDENT: feminine
    3. NUMBER OF ANTECEDENT: singular
    4. SELECTION: **cuánta**
Tengo mucha carne. ¿**Cuánta** quieres?

260

I have a lot of books. ***How many** do you want?*
    1. ANTECEDENT: **los libros** *(books)*
    2. GENDER OF ANTECEDENT: masculine
    3. NUMBER OF ANTECEDENT: plural
    4. SELECTION: **cuántos**
Tengo muchos libros. ¿**Cuántos** quieres?

I have a lot of magazines. ***How many** do you want?*
    1. ANTECEDENT: **las revistas** *(magazines)*
    2. GENDER OF ANTECEDENT: feminine
    3. NUMBER OF ANTECEDENT: plural
    4. SELECTION: **cuántas**
Tengo muchas revistas. ¿**Cuántas** quieres?

270

Pattern (see *Tips for Learning Word Forms,* p. 5)
Flashcards
For review, create a card with a short question illustrating each form.

quién, quiénes   *who, whom*

Practice
1. Write questions using the various Spanish forms.
2. Write Spanish sentences answering questions with "who," "what," "how much" and "how many." Then write the questions for your answers.

ANSWER: **Los estudiantes** estudian en la biblioteca.
            The students study in the library.
QUESTION: **¿Quiénes** estudian en la biblioteca?
            Who studies in the library?

ANSWER: Miran **una película**.
            They are watching a movie.
QUESTION: **¿Qué** miran?
            What are they watching?

ANSWER: María compró **cinco suéteres nuevos**.
            Mary bought five new sweaters.
QUESTION: **¿Cuántos** suéteres nuevos compró María?
            How many new sweaters did Mary buy?

WHAT IS A DEMONSTRATIVE PRONOUN?

A DEMONSTRATIVE PRONOUN is a word that replaces a noun as if   1
pointing to it. The word *demonstrative* comes from *demon-
strate*, to show.

> Choose a suit. *This one* is expensive. *That one* is not.
> antecedent   points to one suit   points to another suit

In English and Spanish, demonstrative pronouns can be used
in a variety of ways.

IN ENGLISH

The singular demonstrative pronouns are ***this (one)*** and
that (one); the plural forms are ***these*** and ***those***.   10

> Here are my suitcases. *This one* is big; *those* are small.
> antecedent   singular   plural

> Choose a book. *Those* are in Spanish; *that one* is in English.
> antecedent   plural   singular

This (one), *these* refer to persons or objects near the speaker,
and *that (one)*, *those* refer to persons or objects further away
from the speaker.

This and *that* are also used to refer to an unspecified   20
object, idea, or previous statement.

> What is *that*?
> the object pointed to is unspecified

> *That* is true.
> refers to an idea previously expressed

IN SPANISH

Demonstrative pronouns are the same words as demonstrative adjectives, except that they are not followed by a
noun. They agree in gender with their ANTECEDENT; that is,   30
the noun to which they refer. Their number depends on
whether they refer to one person or object *(this one, that
one)* or to more than one person or object *(these, those)*.

As pronouns, these words replace the demonstrative
adjective + noun; they agree in number and gender with
the noun replaced.

Here is a chart you can use as reference. (Following the recommendations of the *Real Academia Española* we are not using accent marks on demonstrative pronouns. However, you may still see accent marks on demonstrative pronouns in some textbooks or printed materials.)

TO POINT OUT:	SINGULAR		PLURAL	
	MASCULINE	FEMININE	MASCULINE	FEMININE
ITEMS NEAR THE SPEAKER	este	esta	estos	estas
	this (one)		*these*	
ITEMS NEAR THE THE PERSON SPOKEN TO	ese	esa	esos	esas
	that (one)		*those*	
ITEMS AWAY FROM THE SPEAKER AND PERSON SPOKEN TO	aquel	aquella	aquellos	aquellas
	that one (over there)		*those (over there)*	

To choose the correct form, follow these steps.

1. Determine the location of the item pointed out in relation to the speaker or person spoken to.
2. Find the antecedent.
3. Determine the gender of the antecedent.
4. Determine the number of the antecedent: *this one, that one* → singular; *these, those* → plural.
5. Based on Steps 2, 3 and 4, choose the correct word from the chart above.

Let us apply these steps to some examples.

*Which book do you want? **This one.***
1. RELATIONSHIP: near the speaker
2. ANTECEDENT: *book* (**libro**)
3. GENDER OF THE ANTECEDENT: **libro** → masculine
4. NUMBER OF THE ANTECEDENT: *this one* → singular
5. SELECTION: **este**

¿Qué libro quieres? **Este.**

*Which magazine do you want? **That one.***
1. RELATIONSHIP: near the person spoken to
2. ANTECEDENT: *magazine* (**revista**)
3. GENDER OF THE ANTECEDENT: **revista** → feminine
4. NUMBER OF THE ANTECEDENT: *that one* → singular
5. SELECTION: **esa**

¿Qué revista quieres? **Esa.**

*Which notebooks do you want? **Those (over there).***   80
    1. RELATIONSHIP: away from the speaker and the person spoken to
    2. ANTECEDENT: *notebooks* (**cuadernos**)
    3. GENDER OF THE ANTECEDENT: **cuadernos** → masculine
    4. NUMBER OF THE ANTECEDENT: *those* → plural
    5. SELECTION: **aquellos**
¿Qué cuadernos quieres? **Aquellos.**

*Which suitcases do you want? **These.***
    1. RELATIONSHIP: near the speaker
    2. ANTECEDENT: *suitcases* (**maletas**)
    3. GENDER OF THE ANTECEDENT: **maletas** → feminine
    4. NUMBER OF THE ANTECEDENT: *these* → plural   90
    5. SELECTION: **estas**
¿Qué maletas quieres? **Estas.**

SPANISH NEUTER DEMONSTRATIVE PRONOUNS

Spanish also has three demonstrative pronouns that are
used to refer to an unspecified object, idea, or previous
statement. These pronouns are said to be **NEUTER**; that is,
they have no gender or their gender is not known. These
pronouns are **INVARIABLE**; that is, they do not change form.

esto	*this (one)*	100
eso	*that (one)*	
aquello	*that (one over there)*	

Let us look at some examples.

*What is **this**?*
    Since the antecedent of "this" is unknown, the gender and
    number of the antecedent is also unknown. The neuter
    form must be used.
¿Qué es **esto**?

That's not true.
    The antecedent of "that" is a previous statement which has   110
    no gender. The neuter form must be used.
Eso no es verdad.

*What is **that over there**?*
    Since the antecedent of "that over there" is unknown, the
    gender and number of the antecedent is also unknown. The
    neuter form must be used.
¿Qué es **aquello**?

CHAPTER

47

WHAT IS A RELATIVE PRONOUN?

A **RELATIVE PRONOUN** is a word used at the beginning of a clause that gives additional information about someone or something previously mentioned.

relative clause
additional information about *the book*

I'm reading the book *that* the teacher recommended.

A relative pronoun serves two purposes:

1. As a pronoun it stands for a noun previously mentioned. The noun to which it refers is called the **ANTECEDENT.**

   This is the boy *who* broke the window.

   antecedent of the relative pronoun *who*

2. It introduces a **RELATIVE CLAUSE**; that is, a subordinate clause starting with a relative pronoun (see p. 48 in *What are Sentences, Clauses, and Phrases?*).

   main clause   relative clause

   Here comes the boy *who broke the window.*

   verb   subject subject verb

   The relative pronoun *who* introduces a clause which gives us additional information about the antecedent *boy*.

Relative clauses are very common. We use them in everyday speech without giving much thought as to why and how we construct them. Relative pronouns allow us to combine two thoughts into a single sentence that have a common element, thus avoiding repetition.

SENTENCE A   I met the teacher.

SENTENCE B   He teaches Spanish.

COMBINED   I met the teacher *who* teaches Spanish.

When sentences are combined with a relative pronoun, the relative pronoun can have different functions in the relative clause: it can be a subject, a direct object, an indirect object, or an object of a preposition.

SUBJECT IN A RELATIVE CLAUSE
(see *What is a Subject?*, p. 28)

IN ENGLISH

When functioning as a subject, the relative pronoun used depends on whether the antecedent is a person (human beings and animals) or a thing (objects and ideas).

- PERSON → *who, whom* or *that*

> She is the only student *who* answered all the time.
> She is the only student *that* answered all the time.
> | |
>   antecedent relative pronoun
>   subject of *answered*

- THING → *which* or *that*

> The movie *which* is so popular was filmed in Spain.
> The movie *that* is so popular was filmed in Spain.
> | |
> antecedent relative pronoun
>   subject of *is*

IN SPANISH

When functioning as a subject the same relative pronoun is used for people and things → **que.**

> *John is the student* **who (that)** *answered.*
> Juan es el estudiante **que** respondió.

> *Here is the phone* **which (that)** *isn't working.*
> Aquí está el teléfono **que** no funciona.

DIRECT OBJECT IN A RELATIVE CLAUSE
(See pp. 138-9 in *What are Objects?*)

IN ENGLISH

When functioning as a direct object, the relative pronoun used depends on whether the antecedent is a person or a thing. Relative pronouns functioning as direct objects are often omitted in English (in parentheses below).

- PERSON → *whom* or *that*

> This is the student *(whom)* I saw yesterday.
> This is the student *(that)* I saw yesterday.
> | |
>   antecedent   relative pronoun
>   direct object of *saw*

- THING → *which* or *that*

> This is the book *(which)* Paul bought.
> This is the book *(that)* Paul bought.
> | |
>   antecedent   relative pronoun
>   direct object of *bought*

40

50

60

70

IN SPANISH

When functioning as a direct object, the same relative pronoun is used for people and things → **que**. Unlike English, relative pronouns functioning as direct objects are always expressed in Spanish.

*This is the student (**whom**) John saw last night.*
Este es el estudiante **que** Juan vio anoche.

*This is the book (**that**) John bought.*
Este es el libro **que** Juan compró.

INDIRECT OBJECT AND OBJECT OF A PREPOSITION IN A RELATIVE CLAUSE (see pp. 139-42 in *What are Objects?*)

IN ENGLISH

When functioning as an indirect object or as an object of a preposition, the relative pronoun used depends on whether the antecedent is a person or a thing.

- PERSON → preposition + ***whom***

    This is the student *to whom* I spoke.

    relative pronoun indirect object (object of preposition *to*)

    This is the student *about whom* I spoke.

    relative pronoun object of preposition *about*

- THING → preposition + ***which***

    This is the college *to which* he gave his money.

    relative pronoun indirect object (object of preposition *to*)

    This is the college *about which* he spoke.

    relative pronoun object of preposition *about*

Relative pronouns functioning as indirect objects or as objects of a preposition are often omitted in English. In this case, the preposition, called a **DANGLING PREPOSITION,** is placed at the end of the sentence (see pp. 171-2).

    This is the student *to whom* I spoke.

    relative pronoun indirect object
    This is the student I spoke *to*.

    dangling preposition

    This is the college *about which* he spoke.

    relative pronoun object of preposition
    This is the college he spoke *about*.

    dangling preposition

IN SPANISH

When functioning as an indirect object or as an object of a preposition, the relative pronoun used depends on whether the antecedent is a person or a thing. Unlike English, relative pronouns functioning as indirect objects or as objects of a preposition are always expressed in Spanish. If they have been omitted in the English sentence, you have to restructure the English sentence in order to establish the word order in Spanish.

■ PERSON → preposition + **quien** (sing.) or **quienes** (pl.)

SPOKEN ENGLISH →	RESTRUCTURED
John is the boy	*John is the boy*
I'm going with.	*with whom I'm going.*
preposition	object of preposition *with*

Juan es el chico **con quien** salgo.

SPOKEN ENGLISH →	RESTRUCTURED
The girls I'm writing	*The girls*
to live in Madrid.	*to whom I'm writing live in Madrid.*
preposition	object of preposition *to*

Las chicas **a quienes** les escribo viven en Madrid.

■ THING → preposition + **que**

SPOKEN ENGLISH →	RESTRUCTURED
This is the book	*This is the book*
I was talking about.	*about which I was talking.*
preposition	object of preposition *about*

Este es el libro **de que** hablaba.

SUMMARY

In Spanish, the relative pronoun **que** is used for every function, except as an indirect object or an object of a preposition referring to persons when you would use **quien(es)**.

To handle relative pronouns correctly in Spanish follow these steps:

1. Add the English relative pronoun functioning as an object that may have been omitted.
2. Restructure the English sentence to avoid a dangling preposition.
3. Establish the correct Spanish word order by placing the relative pronoun (preceded by its preposition, if appropriate) right after its antecedent.

Here is a chart you can use as reference:

	PERSON *who, whom, that*	**THING** *which, that*
SUBJECT/DIR. OBJ.	que	que
INDIR. OBJ./ OBJ. OF PREP.	quien(-es)	que

Let's apply the steps outlined above to the following sentences:

*The lady **who** is my neighbor is from Colombia.*
   1. RELATIVE CLAUSE: *who* is my neighbor
   2. FUNCTION OF RELATIVE PRONOUN: subject of relative clause →
      que
   3. PLACEMENT: antecedent *lady (**señora**)* + **que** + clause
La señora **que** es mi vecina es de Colombia.

Here are the books I bought.
RESTRUCTURE: *Here are the books (**that**) I bought.*
   1. RELATIVE CLAUSE: *that* I bought
   2. FUNCTION OF RELATIVE PRONOUN: direct object of relative
      clause → **que**
   3. PLACEMENT: antecedent *books* (**libros**) + **que** + clause
Aquí están los libros **que** compré.

*Peter and Joe are the boys I was talking **to**.* →
RESTRUCTURE: *Peter and Joe are the boys **to whom** I was talking.*
   1. RELATIVE CLAUSE: *to whom* I was talking
   2. FUNCTION OF RELATIVE PRONOUN: object of preposition *to*
   3. PLACEMENT: antecedent *boys* (**chicos**) + **a quienes** + clause
Pedro y José son los chicos **a quienes** hablaba.

Relative pronouns can be tricky to handle; refer to your Spanish textbook for additional rules.[1]

RELATIVE PRONOUNS WITHOUT ANTECEDENTS
Occasionally a relative pronoun does not refer to a specific noun or pronoun. Instead, it refers to an antecedent which has not been expressed or to an entire idea.

IN ENGLISH
A different relative pronoun is used depending on whether it has no specific antecedent or it refers to an entire idea.

---

[1] This handbook does not deal with the forms of **el que, el cual**, or **cuyo** which are usually not included in beginning textbooks.

■ no specific antecedent → **what**

I don't know *what* happened.
          |
   no antecedent
   subject of *happened*

Here is *what* I read.
     |
   no antecedent   210
   direct object of *read (I* is the subject)

■ reference to entire idea → **which**

She didn't do well *which* is too bad.
                 |
   ANTECEDENT: the fact that she didn't do well
   subject of *is*

You speak many languages *which* I envy.
                   |
   ANTECEDENT: the fact that you speak many languages
   direct object of *envy (I* is the subject)   220

IN SPANISH

The same relative pronoun is used when it has no specific antecedent and when it refers to an entire idea→ **lo que**.

Here are a few examples.

What *bothers me most is the heat.*
   1. RELATIVE CLAUSE: what bothers me most
   2. ANTECEDENT: none expressed in the sentence → **lo que**
Lo que me molesta más es el calor.

He doesn't speak Spanish **which** *will be a problem.*   230
   1. RELATIVE CLAUSE: which will be a problem
   2. ANTECEDENT: entire previous clause, *he doesn't speak Spanish*
     → **lo que**
No habla español **lo que** será un problema.

CHAPTER

WHAT ARE INDEFINITES AND NEGATIVES?

Words that refer to persons, things, or periods of time that are not specific or that are not clearly defined are called **INDEFINITES**.

> There was *someone* in the kitchen.
>
> refers to a person that is not specified → indefinite word

Words that deny the existence of persons, things, or periods of time or that contradict ideas or previous statements are called **NEGATIVES**.

> There was *no one* in the kitchen.
>
> denies the existence of a person → negative word

IN ENGLISH

Some common indefinites are *someone, anybody, something, someday.* These indefinite words are often paired with negative words which are opposite in meaning: *no one, nobody, nothing,* and *never.*

INDEFINITES	NEGATIVES
someone anyone	*no one*
somebody anybody	*nobody*
something anything	*nothing*
someday any day	*never*

In conversation indefinites frequently appear in questions while negatives appear in answers.

QUESTION: Is *anyone* coming tonight?
ANSWER: *No one.*

QUESTION: Do you have *anything* for me?
ANSWER: *Nothing.*

QUESTION: Are you going to Europe *someday*?
ANSWER: *Never.*

English sentences can be made negative in one of two ways.

- the word *not* appears before the main verb (see *What are Affirmative and Negative Sentences?*, p. 51)

  > He is *not* working today.
  > I am *not* studying.

- a negative word can be used in any part of the sentence

  > *No one* is coming.
  > He has *never* seen a movie.

English allows only one negative word (either *not* or any of the other negative words) in a sentence. When a sentence contains the word *not*, another negative word cannot be used in that sentence.

> "I am *not* studying *nothing*" [incorrect English]
> | |
>   *not*   negative word
> This sentence contains a double negative: *not* and *nothing*.

When a sentence contains the word *not*, the indefinite word that is the opposite of the negative word must be used (see chart p. 186).

> I am *not* studying *anything*.
> |
> indefinite word opposite of negative word *nothing*

Let us look at another example.

> I have said *nothing* to them.
> |
>   negative word
> *Nothing* is the one negative word.

> I have *not* said *anything* to them.
> |
>   indefinite word
> This sentence contains *not*; therefore, the word *anything* is substituted for *nothing*.

> "I have *not* said *nothing*" [incorrect English]
> | |
>   *not*   negative word
> This sentence contains a double negative: *not* and *nothing*.

IN SPANISH

As in English, the indefinite and negative words exist as pairs of opposites. Here is a chart of the most common indefinites and negatives.

INDEFINITES		NEGATIVES	
something	**algo**	**nada**	*nothing*
some, any	**algún** **alguno**	**ningún** **ninguno**	*none*
someone *somebody*	**alguien**	**nadie**	*no one* *nobody*
someday *always* *sometimes*	**algún día** **siempre** **a veces**	**nunca**	*never*
also, too	**también**	**tampoco**	*not...either*
either, or	**o**	**ni**	*neither...nor*

Contrary to English, an indefinite word cannot appear in a negative Spanish sentence. A negative word, not an indefinite, is used in a Spanish sentence that contains **no** meaning *not*.

No tengo **nada**.

not + negative word *(nothing)*

*I do **not** have **anything**.*

not + indefinite word *(anything)*

The following formula for indefinites and negatives in English and Spanish will help you use them correctly.

> **ENGLISH** → ***not*** + main verb + indefinite word(s)
> **SPANISH** → **no** + verb + negative word(s)

As you can see from the formula above, Spanish requires two negatives in the same sentence. A construction that would be incorrect in English.

No veo a **nadie**.

no + negative word
[word-for-word: *I do **not** see **nobody***]

*I do **not** see **anybody**.*

not + indefinite word

Follow these steps to find the Spanish equivalent of an English sentence with *not* + an indefinite word:

1. Locate the indefinite word in the English sentence.
2. From the chart on p. 186 choose the negative word that is the opposite of the English indefinite word.
3. Restructure the English sentence using *not* + the negative word chosen under 2 above.
4. Put the sentence into Spanish.

Let us apply the steps above to the following sentences.

*I do **not** want to eat **anything**.*   130
      1. IDENTIFY THE INDEFINITE: anything
      2. SELECT THE NEGATIVE: nothing
      3. RESTRUCTURE: "I do *not* want to eat *nothing*"

No quiero comer **nada**.

*I don't (do **not**) know **anyone** here.*
      1. IDENTIFY THE INDEFINITE: anyone
      2. SELECT THE NEGATIVE: no one
      3. RESTRUCTURE: "I do*n't* know *no one* here"

No conozco a **nadie** aquí.

STUDY TIPS — INDEFINITES AND NEGATIVES

Pattern (see *Tips for Learning Vocabulary*, pp. 2-5)
Learn the Spanish indefinites and negatives as pairs of opposites using the chart on p. 188. Notice the following similarities:
- the initial letters for many indefinites is **alg-**
- the initial letter for many negatives is **n-**

Flashcards
Create a flashcard for each of the indefinite and negative words.

    algo   *something*
    nunca   *never*

Practice
1. Sort out the negative cards and look at the English side. Provide the English indefinite word that is the opposite of the negative word on the card.

    never   *sometimes*
    none   *some, any*

2. Sort out the indefinite cards and look at the English side. Provide the English negative word that is the opposite of the negative word on the card.

    something   *nothing*
    someone   *no one, nobody*

3. Repeat steps 1 and 2 referring to the Spanish side of the cards.
4. Write affirmative Spanish sentences with indefinites. Then write the negative of those sentences.

    Vi a **alguien** en el café.   *I saw **someone** in the café.*
    No vi a **nadie** en el café.   *I didn't see **anyone** in the café.*